19th Century
Embroidery Techniques

19th Century
Embroidery Techniques

GAIL MARSH

GUILD OF MASTER
CRAFTSMAN PUBLICATIONS

First published 2008 by
Guild of Master Craftsman Publications Ltd
Castle Place, 166 High Street,
Lewes, East Sussex BN7 1XU

ISBN 978-1-86108-561-0

A catalogue record for this book is available from
the British Library.

Associate Publisher: Jonathan Bailey
Production Manager: Jim Bulley
Managing Editor: Gerrie Purcell
Editor: Virginia Brehaut
Managing Art Editor: Gilda Pacitti
Designer: Chloë Alexander

All photographs by Martyn Pearson except:
pages 8 and 9 © RBKS Collections.

Set in Arrus BT and Shelley Volante BT

Colour origination by GMC Reprographics
Printed and bound in China by Hing Yip Printing Co. Ltd.

Embroidery Techniques

- *Canvas work*
- *Surface embroidery*
- *Whitework*
- *Patchwork and appliqué*
- *Fancy work*
- *Learning to sew*

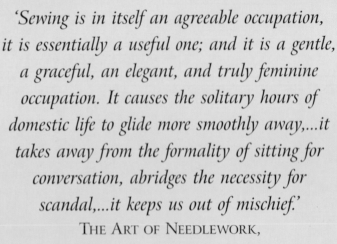

'Sewing is in itself an agreeable occupation, it is essentially a useful one; and it is a gentle, a graceful, an elegant, and truly feminine occupation. It causes the solitary hours of domestic life to glide more smoothly away,...it takes away from the formality of sitting for conversation, abridges the necessity for scandal,...it keeps us out of mischief.'

THE ART OF NEEDLEWORK,
The Countess of Wilton, 1840

Canvas Work

'Of fancy work I knew nothing but what I gathered from my pupil and my own observation; but no sooner was I initiated, than she made me useful in twenty different ways: all the tedious parts of her work were shifted on to my shoulders; such as stretching the frames, stitching in the canvas, sorting the wools and silks, putting in the grounds, counting the stitches, rectifying mistakes, and finishing the pieces she was tired of.'

AGNES GREY, Anne Brontë, 1846

IN the 19th century, needlework was the most popular pastime of the female leisured classes. It was usual for upper- and middle-class homes to employ numerous servants to take care of the everyday running of the home, including food preparation, laundry and care of the children.

The ladies of the house would occupy their time with absorbing hobbies such as watercolour painting, reading, singing, playing the piano, crochet, knitting and colourful needlework. A lady's maid or the laundry servant would be in charge of plain sewing and mending. It was socially acceptable to be occupied at one's embroidery frame, stitching a piece of Berlin wool work, when expecting or indeed entertaining visitors. Designs depicting religious images could be stitched on a Sunday when all other handwork was forbidden. Many a dull afternoon would have been filled with sorting out the threads and stitching a colourful floral spray to grace the drawing room and be admired by all.

Historical threads

The term 'Berlin wool work' was not used until around 1820, when the Berlin patterns had become truly popular. In the mid-1880s Thérèse de Dilmont wrote her *Encyclopedia of Needlework* in association with Dollfus-Mieg et Cie, (DMC) embroidery threads. She titled her chapter on canvas work as 'Tapestry' and this may have been in common usage by this time. Tapestry is not embroidery. It is a woven textile that is worked on a loom. However, this terminology has stayed in use to the present day.

Berlin wool work cushion

1860–1880

18¾ x 18in (47.5 x 46cm)

THIS cushion has a Greek key border surrounding strips of flowers worked in wool and silks. These strips are worked in cross stitch and are separated by lines of closely worked herringbone stitch.

A randomly dyed thread, shading from cream to deep crimson is used for the herringbone. The double canvas has five stitches to each ³⁄₈in (1cm). Close herringbone stitch (see page 25 for details) is worked as a filling on this cushion. The same stitch is used to construct plush stitch (see page 31). It can be worked over any number of canvas threads vertically, but it is best to work into every hole horizontally to cover the canvas.

Berlin wool work cushion, 1860–1880.

A hand-painted design by LW Wittich of a young boy on a country walk, mid-19th century.

Berlin wool work patterns

'The style of modern embroidery, now so fashionable, from the Berlin patterns, dates from the commencement of the present century. About the year 1804–5, a print-seller in Berlin, named Philipson, published the first coloured design, on checked paper, for needlework. In 1810, Madame Wittich, who being a very accomplished embroideress, perceived the great extension of which this branch of trade was capable, induced her husband, a book and print-seller of Berlin, to engage with it with spirit. From that period the trade has gone on rapidly increasing.'

THE ART OF NEEDLEWORK, The Countess of Wilton, 1840

The Countess of Wilton's words, written in 1840, noted the middle of a veritable craze that would last well into the 1870s. Indeed the love of this form of needlework still exists today in the form of kits complete with printed canvas and selected threads. When Frau Wittich encouraged her husband, LW Wittich, to print Berlin wool work patterns, little did she know that by the 1840s there would be up to 1,400 designs available for sale. Other notable designers and printers were Carl F Wicht, Hertz and Wegener and GE Falbe.

The patterns were engraved onto copper plates and printed onto point (graph or squared) paper. Each small square representing one stitch contained a symbol indicating which colour of wool to use. The patterns were hand-coloured using watercolour paint, following the symbols. A small block of each colour used was painted down the side of the point paper for

Historical threads

Berlin wool work patterns changed noticeably over the period 1830–1880. Floral designs in the 1830s and 1840s were subtle coloured bouquets, posies or possibly wreaths, usually with pale, neutral backgrounds. During the 1840s there was an interest in textured techniques such as black lace effects, plush work and Florentine patterns.

By the 1850s larger and more exotic flowers appeared such as lilies, full-blown tulips and large moss roses. The floral bowers often included a foreign bird taken from contemporary publications such as Audubon's *Birds of America*. These designs were placed on black, red or bright blue backgrounds.

The 1850s and 1860s saw the craze for beads sewn on canvas, either combining beads with wool work as in Grisaille work or using different coloured beads over all the canvas. By the late 1860s and 1870s the colour schemes were becoming more muted again. Flowers gave way to geometric patterns.

Throughout the whole Berlin wool work era pictures were always popular, just as 'tapestry' images are today. Medieval scenes, the peasant in the idyllic countryside, religious themes and the Royal family and their pets were all stitched with enthusiasm.

Chair back
circa 1860
17¼ x 25½in (44 x 64.5cm)

Tʜɪs exotic floral design is worked in half-cross stitch on single canvas, six stitches to ³/₈in (1cm). The black background is worked in basket weave stitch. The flower highlights are worked in silk thread.

Detail of the chair back.

Banner fire screen
circa 1860
13½ x 15in (34.5 x 38cm)

Aɴ all-over flower and leaf design embroidered in cross stitch on Penelope double canvas, four stitches to ³/₈in (1cm). The white flowers are worked in white, grey and clear glass beads sewn with beige sewing cotton. The centres of the other flowers and the leaf highlights are stitched with silk thread. The use of the new aniline dye colours of violet and magenta are used with great effect against the black background.

Banner fire screen showing the vibrant aniline dye colours against black.

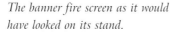

The banner fire screen as it would have looked on its stand.

Canvas

There was a good choice of canvas available in the repositories, both single or double weave and in every thread count from the finest to coarse rug canvas. Berlin canvas was woven from silk thread wound around a cotton core. It was a single or mono canvas and was so attractive that the background could be left unworked. It was very delicate and could only be used for decorative items.

- 'German' canvas had every tenth thread coloured yellow for ease of counting out the pattern.
- 'Java' or jute canvas was used for heavy items like rugs and carpets.
- 'Bolting' was a wool canvas often used for children's samplers.

The double-weave canvas, called 'Penelope', was invented around 1830 and was much easier to work on, as the stitching holes were woven larger than those being stitched over. It was available in different qualities and ranged from three to thirty stitches per 1in (25mm). Penelope canvas had the advantage of being able to accommodate two stitch sizes. By stitching in every hole, half-sized stitches could be made. This was useful for fine detail such as faces. The creation of Penelope canvas at the same time as the patterns were flooding the market helped Berlin wool work to become more fashionable.

The same designs could be used on any gauge of canvas so long as a suitable weight of thread was used. With fine canvas the embroiderer would produce a small, delicate item and the coarse canvas produced a large piece of work.

'The size of the canvas used for Berlin Wool Work must depend on whether single or double wool is to be used, the space to be covered and whether the stitch is to be taken over one or two threads.'

THE DICTIONARY OF NEEDLEWORK, SFA Caulfield & BC Saward, 1885

Canvas work memo book cover

1837

5¼ x 4in (13.5 x 10cm)

THE cover of this book is made of fine silk canvas and is worked with cross stitch motifs in silk threads. The book is lined with cream moiré silk. The front has two doves parting but joined with a lover's knot. The back has the floral motif and the dainty border continues up the spine. The inside cover has the inscription, 'Wm. Peel from his sincere friend Elizabeth Peach Leghorn, August 31st 1837.' It is presumed that the photograph opposite is of Mr W Peel.

Memo book cover on fine silk canvas, 1837.

The inside cover is inscribed to Wm. Peel.

Detail of two angels

THIS large piece of canvas work is worked in beads and Berlin wool work. The faces and hands are worked in 'petit point', meaning small stitch. The double canvas can accommodate twice as many stitches if every hole in the canvas is utilized and this characteristic is very useful for portraying faces or other small details. The background has a count of five beads or stitches to ³⁄₈in (1cm) and the faces have ten stitches to ³⁄₈in (1cm).

Detail of beaded angels with face and hands worked in 'petit point'.

Frames and equipment

A frame was essential for canvas work. However, looking at surviving examples it was not often utilized. Both tent and half-cross stitch distorted the canvas from a square shape to a parallelogram. Although this distorion could have been corrected by dampening the work and stretching and pinning it back into shape, it could have been avoided completely by using a frame in the first place.

A traditional slate frame was preferred as the canvas would have been too thick for an embroidery hoop. The frames came in two types with slightly different stretching mechanisms, pegs or screws. The canvas was stitched to the tape on the top and bottom rollers. These were held apart with laths held with pegs or discs that screwed on to turned laths. The sides of the canvas were firmly laced to the laths. Thus the embroiderer could work with two hands, one above and one below. Although it took two movements to complete a stitch, the stitches were even and there was no distortion. The frames were supported on legs, which were arranged at a suitable height for working at when seated on a chair. If the frame lacked legs, it could be propped against a table and supported against the waist, again leaving both hands free to stitch. The other equipment needed was a packet of needles, latterly called 'tapestry' needles, which had a long eye to accommodate the wool thread and a blunt point, and a pair of small scissors to snip off the thread ends.

'The canvas is tightly stretched in a frame, so that the selvedges come to the braced sides.'
The Dictionary of Needlework, SFA Caulfield & BC Saward, 1885

'At length I was called upon, one fine morning, to accompany her in a walk to the village. Ostensibly she went to get some shades of Berlin wool, at a tolerably respectable shop that was chiefly supported by the ladies of the vicinity: really – I trust there is no breach of charity in supposing that she went with the idea of meeting with the Rector himself, or some other admirer by the way...'
Agnes Grey, Anne Brontë, 1840

Frames suitable for Berlin wool work

1 A screw mechanism frame clamped to adjustable legs.

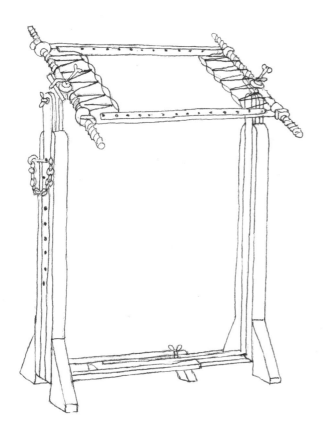

2 A traditional slate frame with stretchers and pegs.

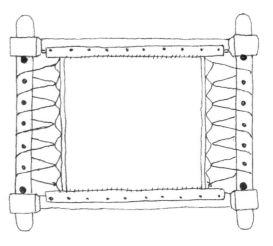

3 A small-sized screw mechanism frame.

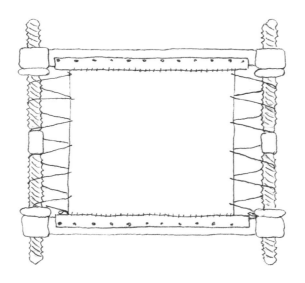

The basic Berlin wool work stitches

Cross stitch

Most pieces of Berlin work are worked in cross stitch. It can either be worked in rows, slanting one way and crossing on the way back or as individual stitches.

Detail of Berlin wool work cushion cover, 1850–1860 worked in cross stitch.

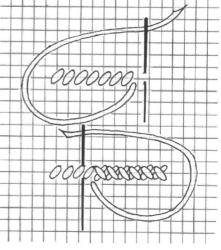

Half-cross stitch

This stitch can be recognized by the straight stitch on the back of the work. It is more economical with thread than cross or tent stitch but the wool must be thick enough to cover the canvas with a single row.

Detail of chair back circa 1860 with floral design worked in half-cross stitch.

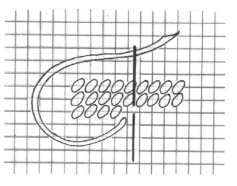

Tent stitch

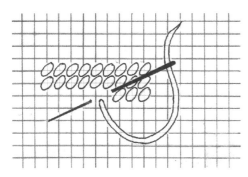

This stitch looks the same as half-cross stitch but on the back of the work there is a large slanting stitch. Tent stitch appears to cover the canvas more fully than half-cross stitch.

Detail of slipper tops 1865–1875 with beige flowers worked in tent stitch.

Basket weave stitch

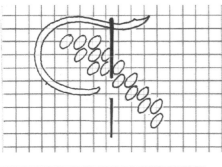

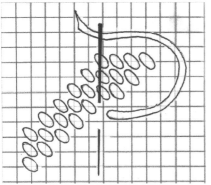

So called because the back of the work has the appearance of basket weaving. The stitch is worked in diagonal rows going down and then coming back up. Although it looks exactly the same as half-cross and tent stitch, it does not distort the canvas shape. It is a useful stitch for large areas of plain background.

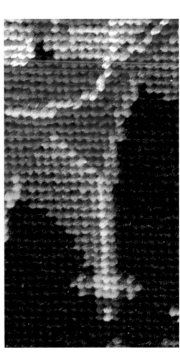

Detail of chair back circa 1860 with background worked in basket weave stitch.

Herringbone stitch

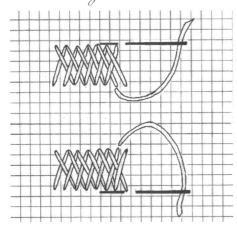

Herringbone stitch is often used as a filling stitch. It can be used over any number of canvas threads vertically, but horizontally it is best to work in every hole to cover the canvas.

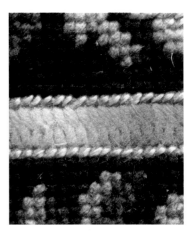

Detail of striped rose cushion. The stripes are worked in herringbone stitch.

Youth's waistcoat

circa 1845

Chest 34in (86.5cm)

THIS smart waistcoat must have looked very fashionable in its time. One stripe is composed of a red cross and a green diagonal block worked in straight stitches using adjacent holes of the single canvas. The second is in cross stitch worked over two canvas threads. The stripes are separated by narrow lines of horizontal green stitches, which are outlined with white silk back stitch. The canvas has 11 threads per ¾in (2cm).

The waistcoat back is made of glazed cotton and the whole garment is lined with the same cloth. There are flaps inset in the waist side seams with two eyelets each. These would have been laced at the back waist to ensure a neat fit. The mock pocket bands and six buttonholes complete the stylish front.

The stitchwork on the waistcoat. The graph paper lines represent the weave of the canvas threads.

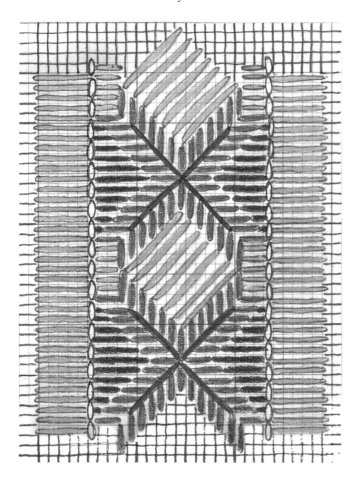

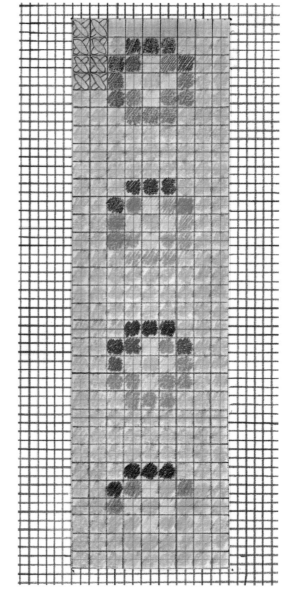

Drawing of the waistcoat.

Detail of the waistcoat showing the stripe pattern.

Slipper tops

1865–1875

Length 12in (31cm)

WORKED on purple Penelope canvas, five stitches to ³⁄₈in (1cm), this slipper top has roses and poppies worked in velvet stitch using every hole of the canvas. The pile has been trimmed and shaped to look like sculpted petals. The leaves are worked in tent stitch and the ground in half-cross stitch. Flowers are worked up the sides of the slippers in tones of beige with silk highlights. The new aniline dyes, Magenta and Solferino, show up well against the black background.

The Englishwoman's Domestic Magazine *printed many patterns of floral slippers for ladies and gentlemen.*

Slipper tops embroidered with velvet stitch floral motifs.

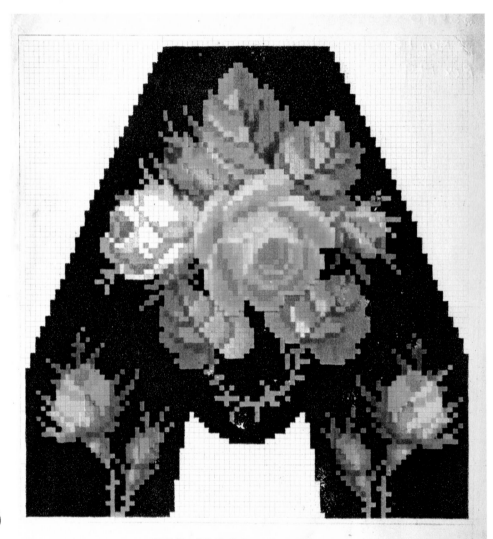

THE FLORAL SLIPPER
For Ladies or Gentlemen
Expressly designed and prepared for
the Englishwoman's Domestic Magazine

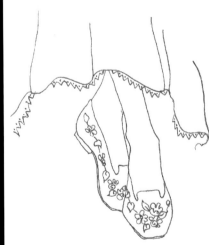

A detail of the floral slippers.

Although these slippers have a feminine design, they were often made with similar patterns for gentlemen. The 'Floral Slipper' pattern for Ladies or Gentlemen expressly designed and prepared for *The Englishwoman's Domestic Magazine* illustrates this exactly.

The slipper tops would be carefully embroidered and sent to a cobbler or shoemaker to be made up and soled. Sometimes slippers such as these were sold as kits, often with the motifs ready worked, leaving the embroiderer only having to stitch the background.

Velvet stitch

1   Worked over two canvas threads.
    Bring the needle up at *A* and down at *B*.

2   Bring the needle up at *A* again.

3   Take the needle down at *B* and up at *C*,
    holding the thread loop with the thumb.

4   Take the needle down at *D* to secure the loop.

5   When finished stitching the area required, cut
    the loops and trim and shape the pile.

6   To make the loops evenly sized, work them over
    a knitting needle or gauge.

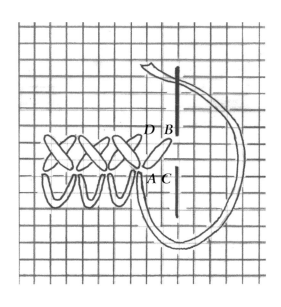

Stool top

1840–1860

12¾ x 14¼ x 4in (32.5 x 36.5 x 10cm)

THIS stool top has been embroidered with plush stitch. The deep pile produced has been trimmed and shaped into little square cushion shapes. These are separated by a cross stitch grid which is the first row of the technique. The careful use of the coloured threads has produced a marbled effect. The sides of the stool are worked in cross stitch with a scroll design echoing the colours of the plush. The canvas is coarse count being two cross stitches per ³⁄₈in (1cm). The stool edges have been trimmed with red cotton cord. The needlework shops offered a professional trimming service for plush and velvet work for the discerning embroiderer.

Plush-stitched stool top,
1840–1860.

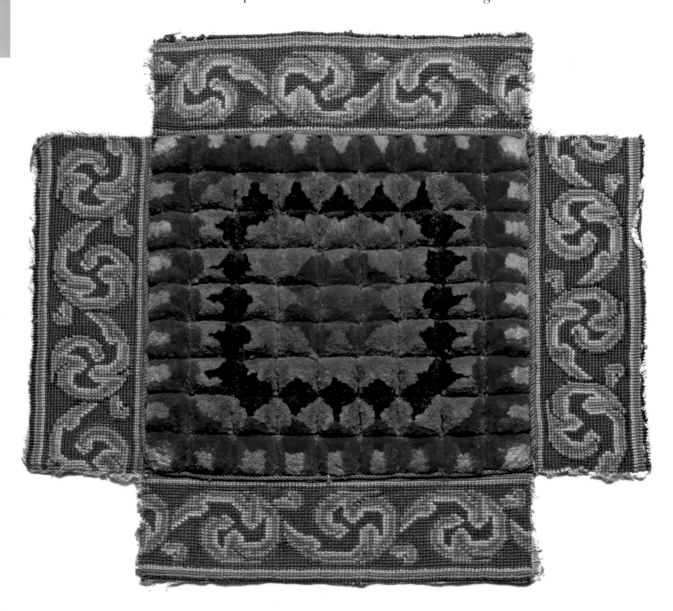

Detail of the plush-stitched stool top.

Footstool worked in plush stitch.

Plush stitch

1   Work a row of cross stitch over two canvas threads.

2   Cover this with a narrow strip of card.

3   Work a row of close herringbone stitch, one canvas thread either side of the cross stitch.

4   Work another row of close herringbone stitch over the last row. The thread can be used double for the herringbone stitches. This stage can be repeated as often as required.

5   Slide the tip of the scissor blades along the strip of card and cut the herringbone stitches to form the pile. The inner rows will be shorter than the outer rows and the 'plush' can be trimmed to take advantage of the natural shape.

The Young Ladies Journal advises steaming the work over boiling water to lift the pile and painting the back with strong gum to fix the stitches.

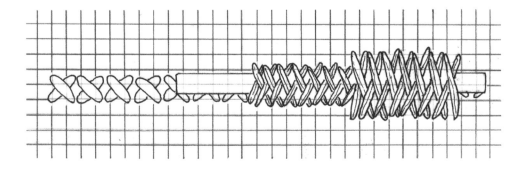

Needlework box samplers

Although the majority of Victorian canvas work pieces are worked in cross, half-cross and tent stitch, a fascinating range of different stitches and techniques can be found on the samplers worked by professional or competent embroiderers. Not to be confused with the alphabet samplers produced by young children, these samplers are usually long and narrow and the edges are often bound with silk or cotton ribbon. They appear to have been kept rolled up in the needlework box and solely been used to record interesting patterns, stitches and colour combinations. They show a variety and interest in texture and design that is lacking in the canvas work pieces made for public display.

Made between 1835 and 1870, the only guide to dating these pieces is the introduction of chemical dyes. The bright magenta and crimson colours were in general use by the 1860s. Otherwise the samplers all seem to be a pleasing mixture of quaint motifs and geometric patterns stitched as the owner discovered them.

Sampler one

mid-19th century

7½ x 27¾in (19.5 x 70.5cm)

MADE of single linen canvas, 12 threads per ³/₈in (1cm), this sampler is bound on all sides with dark green bias binding. It is lined with pale blue cotton fabric. There are over 40 small cross stitch motifs and patterns. Other techniques shown are striped plush stitch, a lace effect and a florentine design. The small florentine pattern is stitched in shades of rose pink and golden beige. The straight stitch always goes over four canvas threads and drops in steps of two canvas threads. Each diamond-shaped section is completed before moving on to the next, to avoid miscounting.

The complete sampler showing many different techniques.

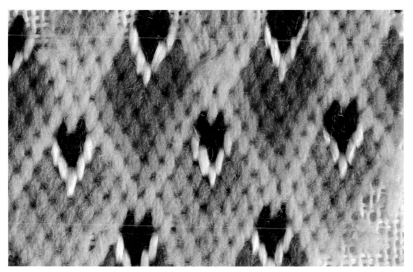

A detail of the florentine pattern.

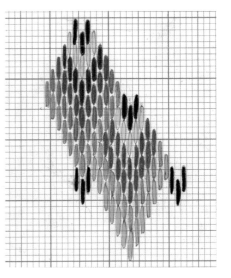

Straight stitch for the florentine pattern.

A variation of plush stitch featured on the sampler.

Also featured is another variation on plush stitch. Two rows of cross stitch, each over two canvas threads, are worked first. Then a row of close herringbone stitch is worked over the cross stitch with some red wool thread. The herringbone stitches are carefully cut up the middle and they spring back to form a pile strip and reveal the cross stitches again. The technique produces a texture somewhat similar to corduroy fabric.

A detail of one of the cross stitch border patterns.

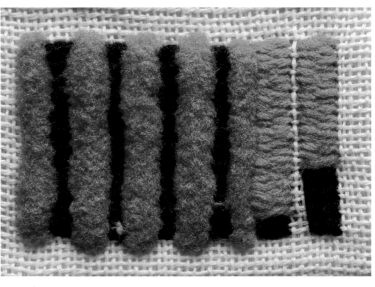

The complete sampler.

Detail showing this simple geometric pattern enhanced with tiny glass beads.

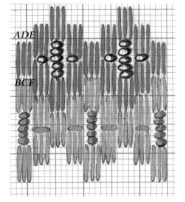

*Beaded geometric detail. For economy of thread, the needle follows the path of **A–B**, up at **C**, down at **D**, up at **E** and so on – thus there is no wastage on the wrong side.*

Sampler two
1860–1870
17½ x 10½in (44.5 x 26.5cm)

THIS sampler, worked on single canvas 12 threads per ³⁄₈in (1cm), has three edges hemmed with slip stitch and the remaining edge is the selvedge. There is a delightful red and cream geometrical pattern using small glass beads sewn on with sewing cotton. Every stitch is worked over six canvas threads and steps up half a block every three stitches. The small peach stitches are silk.

There is also a neat diagonal pattern in the same threads with the addition of turquoise. The vertical stitches are worked over five threads of canvas and step down one canvas thread each stitch. Six stitches are worked, then the block is repeated.

Detail of a simple but effective geometrical pattern worked in three colours.

*For economy of thread, the embroiderer followed the path **A–B**, up at **C**, to **D**, up at **E** and so on – thus taking small diagonal stitches.*

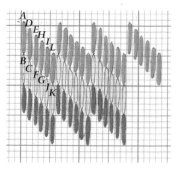

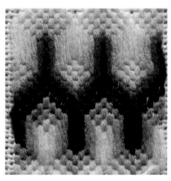

Detail showing the florentine pattern.

Establish the sequence of the pattern by working the black row of stitches first, then stitch the rest above and below this line.

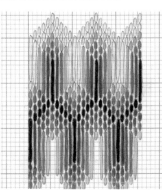

Sampler three

mid-19th century

9¼ x 6¼in (23.5 x 16cm)

T HREE frayed edges and one selvedge surround this sampler made of cotton canvas eight threads to ³/₈in (1cm). The stitch patterns are marked with Indian ink A–E. A florentine pattern has vertical stitches that are always worked over two or ten canvas threads. A small textural stitch neatly stitched in red, cream and turquoise is worked over four canvas threads.

The complete sampler.

Detail showing the diagonal textural stitch worked in bands of graduating colours.

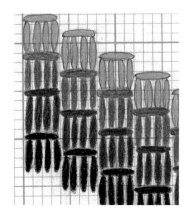

Four stitches are worked vertically alongside one another and then finished by the fifth stich worked horizontally across the top.

35

CASE STUDY

Lace effects on canvas

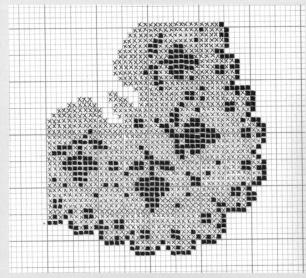

Graphed pattern of the black lace-effect design.

Detail of the delicate 'black lace' stitching.

Detail from sampler one (see page 32), showing a simple but effective black lace design. To add to the delicacy of the pattern, little straight stitches have been added to the top edge and the scallop, hinting at a picot finish.

The above border charted on graph paper.

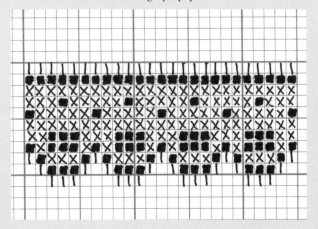

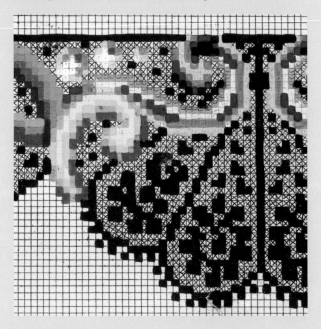

Detail of a hand-painted design for black lace-effect canvas work designed by T Bermann for John Kunsthändler, No 881.

Cushion cover or tablemat

1835–1850

14½ x 15¼in (37 x 39cm)

This very clever canvas work technique produces an effect like black bobbin lace. The black motifs are worked in cross stitch using the normal wool thread. The ground is filled in with cross stitch too, but a fine silk thread is used so that the canvas shows through the stitching. Some examples of this 'lace work' use black sewing cotton for the background. The coloured part of the design is worked in cross stitch in subtle shades of early Berlin wools.

The single canvas is very fine, being ten threads per ³⁄₈in (1cm) and of a good even quality. The area between the border and the centre motif has been left unworked.

Beadwork

Beads stitched on canvas in lieu of a wool stitch appears to have become popular in the mid-1850s and continued well into the 1880s until canvas work in any form was completely out of favour. The same Berlin wool work patterns could be used – but one square representing one stitch was now replaced by one bead. The floral and geometric patterns were the favourites. Although a mixture of the beadwork with fine detail and backgrounds worked in wools continued to be in fashion. A large piece covered entirely with beads could be very heavy!

Kits could be purchased with beading already worked, so the needlewoman only had to fill in the wool background. Steel beads were used for outlining motifs but unfortunately these have usually rusted with time. Pearl beads were occasionally used for highlights and special effects.

Beadwork was found on all the usual artefacts of the Victorian home, like footstools, tea trays, fire screens, tea cosies and valances. Watch pockets, which were made to hang near the bed for storing one's watch overnight, were a popular gift.

The beads were made from glass. The molten glass was drawn out into fine tubes, which were cut into bead-sized pieces. The glass was washed in revolving barrels, which removed the impurities and rounded off the shape. Colours were added at this process or at the initial glass-making stage. Finally the beads were heated up again and, by passing them over abrasive stones, they were polished to a shiny finish. They were then sieved to grade into sizes. Victorian ladies owned partitioned bead boxes to store the various colours and sizes separately.

Using a strong, sewing thread, the stitch is basically the half-cross stitch with a bead threaded onto the needle before each stitch. To have the beads slope in the same direction as the wool work stitches it is necessary to make the bead stitch slope in the opposite direction. A fine sewing needle is required to pass through the hole in the bead.

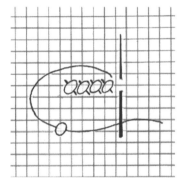

Historical threads

The beads came from Italy and France and were made of glass. Later on in the century, they were manufactured in the English Midlands, but these were said to be not as fine a quality as the European beads. They were bought from the warehouses and repositories by weight were often referred to as 'pound' beads. They were available in small sizes for fine canvas, knitting and crochet, medium sizes for canvas work and large for furnishing trimmings. Black, shades of grey, opaque white and clear were used for the fashionable 'Grisaille' work, the name taken from the term for monochrome, shaded artwork. This Grisaille work often had plain wool backgrounds, which ideally complemented the subtle grey designs. A huge variety of coloured beads were available, in clear and opaque, and these were used for completely beaded designs.

Beaded Footstool

1850–1870

Diameter 16in (41cm)

A circular piece of beadwork made for the upholstered cushion of a small footstool. The waterlilies are entirely stitched with brightly coloured beads and the water is filled with cross stitch in shades of turquoise wools. The beads are small and the canvas fine, there being six beads per ³/₈ in (1cm).

Tea cosy

1880

9½ x 16in (24 x 41cm)

THIS patterned tea cosy is worked in shades of grey, white, black, amber and clear beads. The leaves are worked in cross stitch in shades of green and the background is pale blue. The embroiderer has lost track of her stitches and some of the leaves have the stitches sloping in the wrong direction. It is very heavy, densely padded and lined with black satin. It is worked on single canvas, five beads to ³/₈in (1cm).

Surface embroidery

'Practical instructions in the Art of Embroidery
have been rendered necessary by the revolution in needlework
that has taken place during the last few years.
Berlin wools have been supplanted by crewels,
and cross stitch and tent stitch are superseded by that
used in the old tapestries.'
ART NEEDLEWORK, THE HOME HELP SERIES, 1877

When Victorian ladies became bored with the repetitive stitches of Berlin wool work, they welcomed the next embroidery craze called 'Art Needlework'. The new designs and motifs were curvaceous and often drawn from nature. The influences of William Morris, who believed that designing in general had become too industrial and mechanical due to mass production, led to a yearning for medieval craftsmanship and traditional techniques. Thus 'Art Needlework' was more difficult to work than mechanically following a graphed pattern with cross stitches. It required a certain skill to stitch a free-flowing design with evenly embroidered surface stitches and gain the desired effect of 'painting with the needle'.

'It is not worth doing unless it is very copious or very delicate – or both...and also since we are using especially beautiful materials, that we shall make the most of them and not forget that we are gardening with silk and gold thread.'

HINTS ON PATTERN DESIGNING, William Morris, from a lecture in 1881

Circular embroidered panel, 1895

Diameter 11½in (29cm)

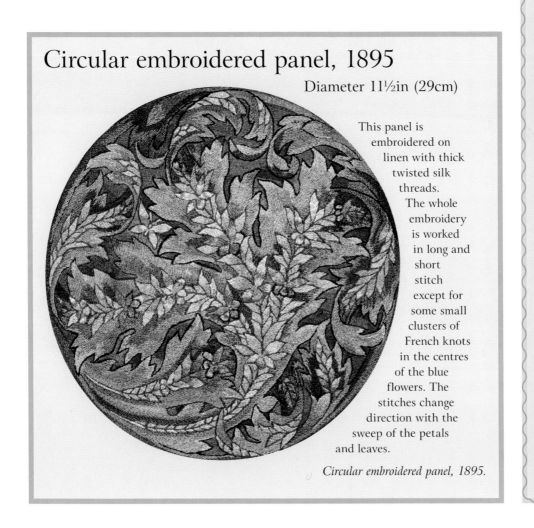

This panel is embroidered on linen with thick twisted silk threads.

The whole embroidery is worked in long and short stitch except for some small clusters of French knots in the centres of the blue flowers. The stitches change direction with the sweep of the petals and leaves.

Circular embroidered panel, 1895.

Square panel and detail, 1895.

Square panel

1895

20½ x 21¾in (52 x 55cm)

THIS panel, possibly a cushion, of cotton fabric was ready-printed with a brown outline of the design. The thread is a rich, thick, loosely twisted silk, which is hand-dyed. The main motifs are outlined in red stem stitch and the whole fabric is covered with darning stitch. The stitches follow the contours of the stems and petals. The stamens of the flowers are worked in satin stitch.

Designs: tracing and transferring to fabric

Many designs for Art Needlework were available in needlework books, magazines and 'Shilling Guides' (small booklets priced at one shilling). However, a little artistic drawing skill was advantageous. It was suggested that the embroiderer drew from nature, used curves and composition and observed the Japanese traditions of placing motifs asymmetrically on the surface of the fabric. Other advice warned not to mix styles and eras, keep a natural balance and used the maxim 'less is more' to produce an aesthetically pleasing design.

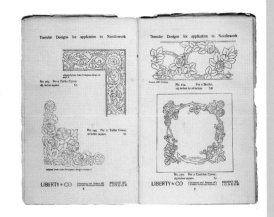

Iron-on transfer designs available from Liberty's of London at the end of the century.

'Flowers, ferns and leaves &c., require little exactitude of form and size, and a lady with little or no talent may easily effect them with the barest knowledge of drawing.'
ART NEEDLEWORK, A COMPLETE MANUAL, 1882

The design could be drawn directly onto the fabric, but if the embroiderer was not confident with freehand drawing then she may prefer to sketch onto paper first or use a commercial pattern. By holding the drawing against a window in daylight, the image could be traced onto tracing paper. The fabric was spread flat with transfer paper placed faced down and the tracing on top and fixed in position with pins. The lines were then traced over with a blunt needle or a stylus.

'There is a tracing apparatus invented by Mr Francis, 16 Hanway Street, Tottenham-Court-Road, London...The cloth is prepared in two colours, white and blue. The blue is suitable for light materials, the white for dark. A piece of cloth of each colour, and blue and white pencils, together with full instructions for use, are supplied by the inventor.'
ART NEEDLEWORK, A COMPLETE MANUAL, 1882

Alternatively the traditional 'prick and pounce' method would be used. The lines on the paper design were pricked with a sharp pin or needle. The paper was laid over the fabric and pinned in place. Pounce powder was dabbed over the lines. Pounce was made of pulverized pipe clay for white lines or the same powder mixed with charcoal for dark lines. The powder was contained in a small saucer and was applied with a roll of felt or a stencil brush, known as a 'Poonah brush'. The paper design was carefully removed, so as to not disturb the powder dots, and the lines gone over with paint or Indian ink using a fine sable brush. Cobalt blue watercolour, Chinese white paint or sepia ink was recommended, depending on the colour of the background fabric.

Historical threads

An English company, called William Briggs, invented iron-on transfers in 1875. After this date they were often available in ladies' journals and magazines as a free gift and could be purchased from the embroidery repositories or shops such as Liberty's of London. Many household items were bought as traced goods, that is the outline was already printed onto the fabric and ready to be embroidered.

Embroidered panel

1880–1890

20½ x 15½in (52 x 39.5cm)

A spray from a blackberry bush supports a small bird on this silk embroidered brown satin panel. The flowers and leaves are worked in stranded thread and the little bird in twisted silks. The panel was probably intended for a fire screen to cover the empty grate in the summer months. The design is typical of the advice to the embroiderer 'to go out and draw from nature'.

Embroidered panel, 1880–1890.

Fabrics

'The textile fabrics suitable for embroidery are not very numerous, and, with a few exceptions, are exactly similar to those used centuries ago.'
ART NEEDLEWORK, THE HOME HELP SERIES, 1877

The statement above advised the needlewoman to search out traditional fabrics that were a natural or subtly dyed colour. There appears to have been quite a choice and purchasing these fabrics must have been much more exciting than buying canvas.

Various kinds of linen were available, all for different purposes. 'Round towelling' was for beginners and children to stitch on, as it was cheap at four pence per yard. 'Crash' was a very popular grey linen for antimacassars, toilet mats and nightdress cases. 'Tea cloth' linen was dyed in pastel shades for tea cloths and table linen. 'White linen' was the finest quality and recommended for expert needlewomen. 'Twill linen' was tough and very stout and used for curtains and portieres.

Cotton fabric was made in similar weights and qualities. 'Workhouse sheeting' was a thick, coarse twill-weave cotton and used for heavy crewel work. 'Muslin' was a fine cotton for dresses, aprons and blouses. 'Twill cotton' was dyed in a variety of colours and was suitable for curtains and chair covers.

Wool fabrics such as 'serge' and 'cloth' were woven in different thicknesses and were dyed in a good range of rich colours. 'Merino' and 'cashmere' were used for dresses and jackets and usually embroidered with silk threads.

Silk fabrics needed careful treatment and handling. 'Sarnets', a fine silk cloth, needed backing with 'Holland cloth', a fine cotton fabric or paper. 'Repp' and 'diapered' silks were used for ecclesiastical work. The lustrous 'satin' was beautiful when embroidered with floss silk threads. Pile materials such as 'velvets' and 'velveteens' were used for furnishings.

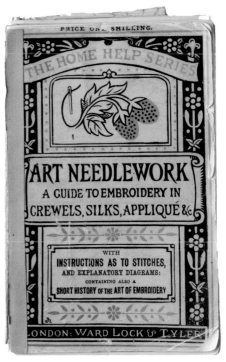

The cover of Art Needlework, *a one shilling guide in* The Home Help Series, *1877.*

Detail of the large oval embroidery worked in wool threads on a 'Crash' background.

Preparation of the fabrics

Fine or loosely woven fabric would be backed with linen or fine Holland. Even paper could be used as a backing material and this was pasted to the back of the fabric.

'Mix some flour and water in a saucepan, add a pinch of alum or resin to every handful of flour. When you have mixed it smoothly, put it on the fire and stir until quite thick. A wooden spoon is the best for this purpose. Paste should not be kept for more than a week. In spreading it on the back of the material it is better to use the fingers rather than a brush, in order that no little lumps get overlooked...The paste should be allowed to dry thoroughly before the embroideress sets to work.'

ART NEEDLEWORK, A COMPLETE MANUAL, 1882

It was advisable to stretch the linen backing in the frame, apply the paste and then smooth the embroidery fabric into position, pressing out any bumps. When using paper, this was applied to the embroidery fabric before stretching.

When the embroidery was completed, the backing material could be cut away close to the stitching. Alternatively, the motifs could be cut out leaving a scant 2–3mm of fabric surrounding the shape. This could then be applied to a ground of velvet or brocade and the edges disguised with an applied cord. This second method was much used on ecclesiastical work or items that would not require draping.

Thin cardboard was used for monograms and 'church work'. The motif was drawn on cardboard and cut out with sharp scissors or a knife. Little 'stays' or connecting bars were retained to keep the correct spacing. The card was tacked to the fabric and then the stays were removed. Not all the Art Needlework projects needed such elaborate preparation. Most of the embroidery was worked in the hand or a small round hoop.

'When a piece of work is finished our paste is brought into requisition to smear over the back...This prevents the ends and fastenings of the silk or wool from coming undone, and effectually keeps the whole 'tidy'.

ART NEEDLEWORK, A COMPLETE MANUAL, 1882

Embroidered monogram

1890

4½ x 4in (11.5 x 10cm)

THIS monogram, initials BMKS, was worked by Lady Blanche Shuttleworth, the mother of Rachel Kay-Shuttleworth. It is worked in silk threads on a linen ground, the shield-shaped background being entirely covered in long and short stitch using cream thread. The initials are worked over a cut cardboard template. The letters are covered with closely worked satin stitch and outlined with couched gold purl.

Embroidered monogram, 1890.

Threads

The most popular threads were made of silk or wool. Crewel wool was two-ply, soft but very strong and very different to Berlin wool in texture and colour. The colours were brilliant without being harsh and were available in an immense range of tints and shades.

'Crewels are the only kind of worsted used for coloured embroidery. They are made with only two plies, and their loose twist causes them, in working, to form lines which may be compared to the lines in copper-plate engraving.'
ART NEEDLEWORK, THE HOME HELP SERIES, 1877

Silk threads were made in many different weights and textures. 'Floss' was available in coarse and fine and had a lovely lustre when worked. 'Dacca', 'Mitorse' and 'Filoselle' were famous brand names. Dacca could be split into separate strands, unlike Floss. Mitorse was the thread used by the Japanese for their exquisite silk embroidery. It was a twisted thread and it was quite a skill to keep the twist even when stitching. Filoselle was a cheaper silk

Detail of a rose worked in floss silk.

thread made from the waste silk cocoons. Sewing silks were usually sold in skeins. Gold and silver threads were expensive and generally only used for church embroidery and ecclesiastical vestments. Silk thread was also comparatively expensive and the Home Help shilling guide states that a 'large supply will soon be available from Australia, reeled and dyed in England'.

Cotton thread was not much in evidence until the late 19th century although the famous DMC company (Dollfus-Mieg et Cie) had been producing a variety of embroidery threads since 1841. These included stranded, pearl cotton, cotton á broder and knitting, crochet and lacemaking threads.

Chenille threads were popular throughout the 19th century. 'Chenille' is French for caterpillar and the thread has a velvety fluffy appearance like its name. Chenille thread, being quite thick, could be embroidered quickly by using a large-eyed, sharply pointed chenille needle.

'Crewels and silks are now made in every shade and tint of colour, so that if the worker has "an artist's eye" for colour she will know exactly what shade to choose as to render her work attractive and artistic'.

ART NEEDLEWORK, A COMPLETE MANUAL, 1882

Detail of a rose worked in chenille thread.

Detail of a lily motif worked in cotton thread.

Hints for working at the frame from
The Home Help Series

1   Cover the lower part of the frame with a soft cloth to avoid friction damage
    from clothing.

2   Surround the actual working area with tissue paper or a soft cloth with a hole
    in it to avoid touching the embroidery.

3   Cover up after a work session to avoid smoke and soot from an open fire.

4   Change body positions to avoid fatigue.

5   Do not work with soiled or worn thread.

6   Check finished work for gaps or missed stitches.

7   Aim for perfection.

Frames, tools and equipment

Fortunately, the frames used for Berlin wool work were also suitable for
Art Needlework. The traditional slate frames were used for stretching
the background fabric. Hand-held round hoops were used for small items
and round hoops with a stand could be clamped to a table.

The needles were the standard round or long-eyed embroidery types, now
being called 'crewel needles' with a sharp point. Embroiderers were advised
to select only the best quality needles.

*'They should be chosen so large as to allow them to carry their needlefulls easily
through the stuff to be embroidered, and the eye should be large enough to take the
thread immediately, and allow of its being drawn backwards and forwards without
distressing it...If you have to tug a needle through the stuff, it is too small and should
be rejected; for tugging spoils material and, besides that, wastes time, strength, and
temper of the worker to a much greater extent than might be generally supposed.'*
THE ART OF NEEDLEWORK, THE HOME HELP SERIES, 1877

The thimble should be old, used and smooth, as a new one could catch on
silk threads. The embroiderer would use two thimbles when working on a
frame, with one hand above and one below. A stiletto, a sharp metal pointed
tool, was used to pierce holes in the fabric to allow bulky couching cords to

be taken to the back of the work. A piercer was also made of metal and was like a stiletto at one end but shaped flat at the other. The flat end was used to smooth stitches or help lay down metal threads and cords.

The hands should be cared for and prepared for a work session:
'...if the fore finger be rough from plain sewing, it should be well rubbed with a pumice stone. In winter the hands should be washed with oatmeal and carefully dried...Remove rings, bracelets and chains as they can catch in your work and can cause fatigue. Rings impede circulation of the fingers.'
ART NEEDLEWORK, THE HOME HELP SERIES, 1877

The needlewoman's dress should be clean and fresh and she should wear a large, clean linen apron with a bib. The sleeves should be covered with linen cuffs and the apron should have a pocket to hold tools and threads.

'Thus attired, your aspect will be far from romantic, but you will be amply repaid for the little sacrifice of personal vanity that you make, by the appearance of your work when finished.'
ART NEEDLEWORK, THE HOME HELP SERIES, 1877

*The round hoop on a stand could be clamped to a table at **A** and the height adjusted at **B**. The screw at **C** altered the angle of the work.*

The basic embroidery hoop could be tightened with a screw mechanism to accommodate any thickness of fabric. To stop the fabric slipping and becoming slack, the inner ring should be bound with a bias strip of fabric or tape.

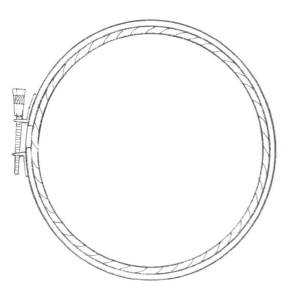

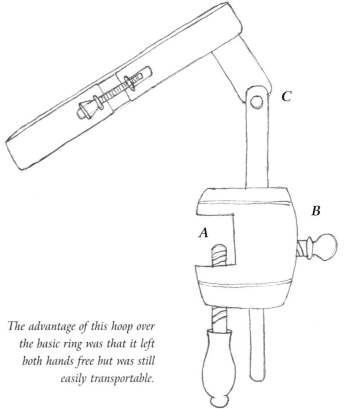

The advantage of this hoop over the basic ring was that it left both hands free but was still easily transportable.

51

The stitches

'The stitch used in crewel work is very old and very simple; but it is the least mechanical of all stitches used in fancy work, and much discretion in its practise is left to the worker; it is like the hatching in chalk and water-colour drawing.'

ART NEEDLEWORK, THE HOME HELP SERIES, 1877

The most basic stitch used in Art Needlework was the straight stitch. In its various forms it could be used as an outline, a solid shape or a delicately shaded filling. Next there are the looped stitches that involve twisting the thread around the needle in some way or another. Although there are literally hundreds of surface stitches, the 19th century embroiderer managed with quite a small repertoire.

If the work was held in the hand, the passing of the needle through the fabric could be done in one movement. If the fabric was mounted in a frame, an up and down needle movement must be used with one hand above the work and one below. This makes the loop and knot stitches a little more difficult to manoeuvre but results in a very even tension.

Stem stitch — an outline or filling straight stitch

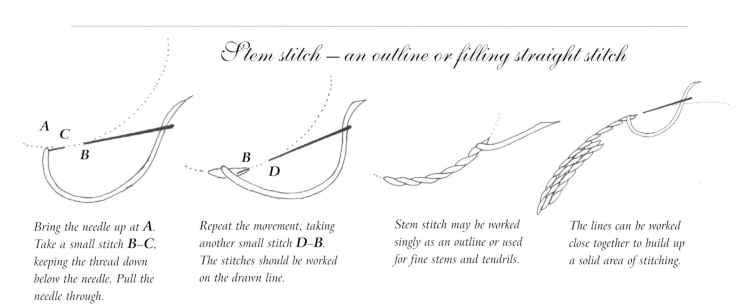

Bring the needle up at **A**. Take a small stitch **B–C**, keeping the thread down below the needle. Pull the needle through.

Repeat the movement, taking another small stitch **D–B**. The stitches should be worked on the drawn line.

Stem stitch may be worked singly as an outline or used for fine stems and tendrils.

The lines can be worked close together to build up a solid area of stitching.

'Stem stitch is so simple that it almost explains itself by diagram. One stitch is laid beyond the other in a continuous line, which should be smooth and even, the thread being always kept on the same side as the needle. It is essentially adapted to work done in the hand; it is used for filling stems and putting in outlines.'

DECORATIVE NEEDLEWORK, May Morris, 1893

Satin stitch — a filling stitch

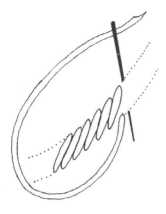

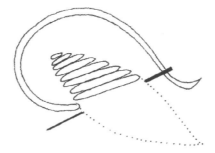

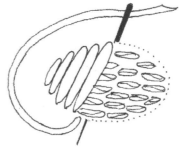

Satin stitch can be used as a broad stem-filling. The straight stitches should have a diagonal slant so that the thread spreads to fill the drawn shape. The skill lies in maintaining a smooth outline whilst keeping the slant of the stitch consistent.

Satin stitch is used to fill larger shapes. Again it is recommended that the stitch slants at an angle, as this gives a better coverage than stitches made at right angles. The edge of the shape should be quite smooth and the tension of each stitch kept even.

Raised satin stitch is sometimes required to give more depth to the embroidery. The area can be 'padded' with little running stitches worked in the opposite direction to the satin stitch, which is worked over this.

'The stitches should be smoothly and evenly laid and should resemble the woof of satin.'
    ART NEEDLEWORK,
    A COMPLETE MANUAL, 1882

Long and short stitch

Also known as crewel stitch and even called feather stitch in the 19th century, long and short stitch was often referred to as 'painting with the needle'.

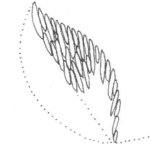

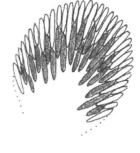

Long and short stitch used as a one-colour filling was the stitch referred to as 'feather stitch' because it looked like the feathers of a bird when well executed. Keeping the outline smooth, straight stitches are worked towards the centre of the motif, each stitch being a different length. The next row interlocks with the first, again keeping the stitch length irregular, so that all the stitches blend into one another.

Long and short stitch was mainly used for the shading of a motif. Keeping the outlines smooth, alternating long and short straight stitches are worked angled to the centre. To maintain a curved shape, extra short stitches may need to be inserted. The next colour dovetails into the gaps of the first row creating a smooth colour transition.

'Naturally a closer stitch and a more solid work are required for antimacassars or sofa cushions, which are always coming in contact with fidgety and restless human beings, decked out with every kind of ornamental excrescence likely to pull and catch at worsted-work, than for a frieze of needlework, nailed immediately under the ceiling.'

ART NEEDLEWORK, A COMPLETE MANUAL, 1882

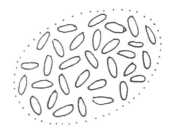

Straight stitches can be used singly as an outline or a decorative texture.

Little straight stitches can be randomly placed to fill a motif. This is called 'speckling'.

Back stitch

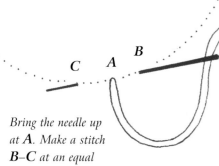

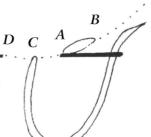

*Bring the needle up at **A**. Make a stitch **B–C** at an equal distance either side of **A**.*

*Repeat the movement making stitch **A–D**.*

The stitches should be worked along the drawn line.

Chain stitch

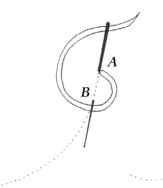

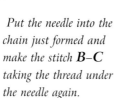

*Bring the needle up at **A** and take a stitch **A–B**, putting the thread under the needle tip. Pull the needle through.*

*Put the needle into the chain just formed and make the stitch **B–C** taking the thread under the needle again.*

Repeat the movement following the drawn line. Chain stitch can be worked as a single line or lines stitched close together to form a filling.

Single or detached chain stitches are now called 'lazy daisy' stitches.

French knots or knotting

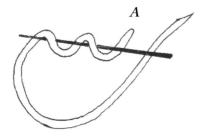

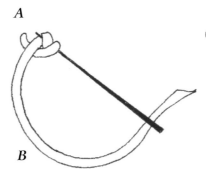

French knots may be worked singly or close together as a filling.

Bring the needle up at A, at the position where the knot is to be. Wrap the needle twice in a clockwise direction.

*Gently tighten the thread twist on the needle and hold with the thumb at **B**. Insert the needle as close as possible to A and take it through to the back of the fabric. Allow the thread to slide through the knot under tension from the thumb so that it sits close to the surface of the fabric.*

'French knots should be as smooth and round as a bead.'

ART NEEDLEWORK, A COMPLETE MANUAL, 1882

Buttonhole or blanket stitch

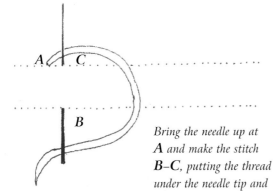

*Bring the needle up at **A** and make the stitch **B–C**, putting the thread under the needle tip and pulling through.*

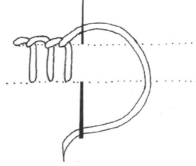

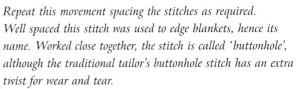

Repeat this movement spacing the stitches as required. Well spaced this stitch was used to edge blankets, hence its name. Worked close together, the stitch is called 'buttonhole', although the traditional tailor's buttonhole stitch has an extra twist for wear and tear.

Darning stitch

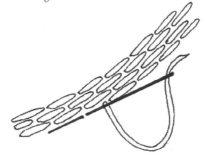

Worked with a thick thread and a loosely woven fabric, darning stitch is only a simple running stitch. The long stitches cover most of the ground by picking up only a couple of fabric threads with each stitch. This is a very economical stitch when using expensive silk threads as only a very little is wasted on the back of the work. It is also very quick to work.

Liberty and Co.

In 1862, a large exhibition of Japanese goods was held in Paris. The display was bought by a English company for their department store in London. Mr Arthur Lazenby Liberty was employed as the manager of this department. Unfortunately, this store closed in 1874 and Mr Liberty saw an opportunity and bought up the bankrupt stock.

In 1875, Liberty's of Regent Street, London, was opened and immediately became the fashionable place to shop. The lacquer-ware, embroidered and printed oriental silks and ceramics did much to influence the 'Japanese style' that became the next 19th century craze.

Liberty's patronized the Arts and Crafts style and commissioned embroidery designs, fabrics and threads from William Morris, the Royal School of Needlework and all the Art Nouveau artists and craftsmen.

Stool top or ottoman lid

1880–1890

26 x 37½in (66.5 x 95cm)

Detail showing the use of various stitches: French knots and satin stitch on the acorns, speckling on the leaves and stem stitch on the tendrils and border.

A large, oval, embroidered piece for use on upholstered furniture. The background fabric is 'crash', the popular grey, hardwearing linen, and the embroidery is worked in wool crewel threads. The colours of the threads are slightly faded.

The stool top or ottoman lid.

Waterlily and bird panel

1890

25 x 52in (64 x 132.5cm)

Tʜɪs cotton panel has a transferred design that is in the Japanese/ aesthetic style made popular by the store Liberty's of London. The embroidery is exquisitely worked in fine crewel wools, showing the art of 'painting with a needle'.

The complete panel.

Detail of the waterlily worked in long and short stitch.

Historical threads

The Aesthetic Movement

In the 1870s, many women rebelled against the corseted fashions of the times and opted for looser, more flowing garments in the shape of smocks that were lightly tied around the waist. These women were notably followers of William Morris and the Pre-Raphaelite Brotherhood of Artists. These romantic garments were available from Liberty's of London and miniature versions were made for children. The dresses often incorporated smocking at the neckline and cuffs.

The Royal School of Needlework

The Royal School of Needlework was opened in 1872 in premises above a bonnet shop in Sloane Street, London. The founders were Lady Welby and Mrs Dolby, both talented needlewomen. The aims were to provide suitable employment for gentlewomen. The only alternative work for an educated young lady at this time was to be a governess. The school started with 20 ladies, some already skilled needlewomen and others apprentices. To become a student at the school, a young lady had to present references from a clergyman and submit samples of her needlework. Married women could participate as outworkers. The average training lasted three years and the ladies had to have means to support themselves throughout this period. Soon after the opening of the school Mrs Dolby died and was replaced by Lady Marion Alford, who later wrote *Needlework as Art* in 1886. As well as commissioned embroideries and repair work, the school prepared packs of traced goods and threads to sell in shops such as Liberty's.

Detail of a double bedcover

1880

Width 13¾in (35cm)

THIS is an early design of the Art Needlework Society and is the border of a bedcover. Sunflowers were all the rage during this period and often appear in one form or another on domestic embroidery. The linen ground is embroidered with fine crewel threads using mainly chain and stem stitch. The centres of the sunflowers are worked in French knots. The colours of the threads are very subtle 'arty colours', that is greens, yellows and rust, as was the fashion for work of this type.

Border from a double bedcover, 1880.

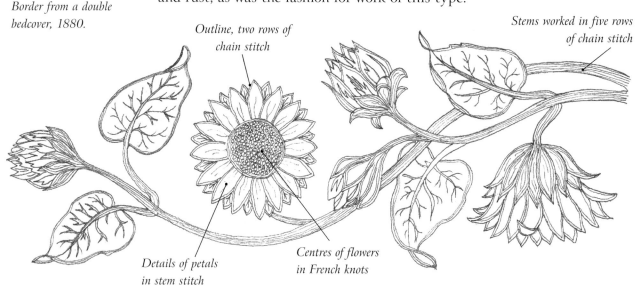

Outline, two rows of chain stitch

Stems worked in five rows of chain stitch

Details of petals in stem stitch

Centres of flowers in French knots

Chenille and wool embroidery

Well before the craze for Berlin wool work and Art Needlework, some very inventive embroidery was being worked on costume. Clothes of the early part of the century were often decorated with chenille, wool or silk embroidery in a style that today looks positively modern.

Chenille and wool were thick threads and were often stitched onto fine silk and muslin fabrics. A large-eyed needle was needed to accommodate the thread. Also the needle would have to be sharp and thick enough to pierce a large enough hole to pull the thread through comfortably. The advantage of these thicker threads was that they were quick to work and required the simplest of straight stitches to create a leaf or a flower.

Chenille embroidered strips
1814–1820

THESE richly embroidered strips are all that remains of two evening dresses of the early 19th century. The thick chenille thread is stitched through the finest silk fabric, requiring only one or two stitches to produce a charming effect. Fine details, such as the thorns on the moss roses were added afterwards with fine silk thread. The chenille threads have retained their strong colours and have not faded with time and wear. Embroidery such as this was usually produced by professional workshops not undertaken as home needlework.

An impression of how the chenille embroidered strips might have been used on early 19th century evening wear. At this time there was a lot of emphasis on the bottom of the skirt and the actual hem was often softly padded to hold out the skirt and display the embroidery.

Details of the chenille embroidered strips.

Child's silk dress
1800–1820

THIS cream silk dress is embroidered with chenille and silk threads. Above the padded hem are dainty sprigs of flowers and leaves, each motif being worked in a different colour combination of pastel pinks, lilacs and blues. The neck edge has a line of couched double strands of chenille. The puffed sleeves are decorated with rosettes made of cream ribbon, gathered tightly on the inside edge and finished with a chenille tassel in the centre. The dress fastens at the centre back with two drawstrings at the neck and waist. There was probably a ribbon sash worn over the waistband.

Detail of the embroidered hem.

Detail of the embroidered neckline trim.

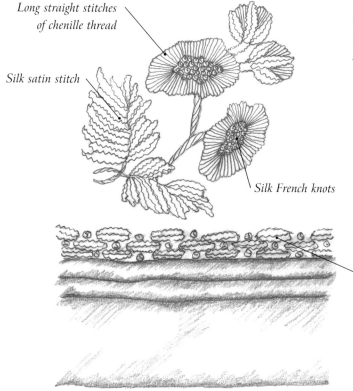

Long straight stitches of chenille thread

Silk satin stitch

Silk French knots

Two strands of chenille thread are couched down with two small silk stitches. The cuff has the same trim

Running stitch with two strands of chenille thread with a silk French knot between each stitch

The hem is softly padded with combed wool and above there are two lines of piping filled with cotton cord

Child's muslin dress

1800–1820

THIS pretty child's dress of fine muslin is embroidered with wool threads in yellow, pale green and bright pink. The daisy-shaped flowers are worked in satin stitch and the narrow hem is covered with three rows of scalloped blanket stitch. The gathered bodice and puffed sleeves have hems decorated with two rows of running stitch, one in the pink wool and the other in the green. The stitches are separated by a yellow French knot in the same style as the hem decoration on the silk dress. The dress fastens at the centre back with drawstrings at the neck and waist.

Detail of the embroidered hem.

The waistcoat as it might have been worn by a 19th century gentleman.

Gentleman's waistcoat

1865–1875

Chest 34½in (88cm)

Ablack satin waistcoat embroidered with chenille and silk threads. The fanciful design of moss roses and thistles is carefully worked using simple straight stitches. The garment is machine-stitched with real welt pockets. The back is black cotton fabric, the whole is lined with tan cotton. There are two side flaps with eyelets in the side seams that would lace at the centre back for a snug fit.

Detail of the waistcoat.

Bandana embroidery

This is a very curious embroidery fashion. Bandanas printed with red, black and cream that have a folk/paisley-type design are embroidered all over using the printed design as a pattern.

'Bandana Handkerchiefs, – Indian washing silk handkerchiefs, having white or coloured spots or diamonds on a red, yellow, blue, or dark ground. They were a yard square, and were both plain and twilled, and kept their colour to the last. Other patterns have long been introduced into their manufacture, and they are extensively imported plain and printed to this country, being solely manufactured for export to the United Kingdom. Imitation Bandanas are largely made in England and elsewhere, but are mostly composed of cotton. They can now be purchased by the yard, and are made into dresses, aprons and caps.'

THE DICTIONARY OF NEEDLEWORK, SFA Caulfield & BC Saward, 1885

Embroidered bandana
1880–1890

THIS cotton bandana has a swirling design worked in satin, stem and long and short stitch using stranded cotton threads. The standard of stitching is exquisite and it almost seems a waste on such a base fabric. The bandana being made of such a flimsy material has been backed with a linen cloth. The embroidery is so dense that it changes a flimsy fabric into one quite heavy and robust. Too stiff to be worn as a shoulder shawl it is presumed that the intended use would be for a table or sideboard cover.

Detail of the embroidered bandana.

CASE STUDY

Leek embroidery

The Wardle Company was based in Leek, Staffordshire, England, and it produced a wide range of silk fabrics and threads. This area of Britain was the centre for most of the silk production at this period. Thomas Wardle asked his wife, Elizabeth, if she could develop some form of embroidery that would make use of his 'tussah' silk fabric and his floss silk threads. William Morris had worked with Wardle and had developed the use of vegetable dyes. The soft, glowing colours were a trademark of Wardle's embroidery threads. Elizabeth chose the type of embroidery popular at this time, which was Art Needlework style.

Leek embroidery can be recognized by its flowers and foliage, often with an Indian influence from Thomas Wardle's travels when he was sourcing raw materials. The natural-coloured tussah silk was block printed with a fine brown outline for the embroiderer to follow. The work used only the basic stitches and on some pieces there was the addition of a couched gold outline.

Elizabeth Wardle set up a school, very much in the style of the Royal School of Needlework, to educate young girls and also to produce embroidered pieces to sell. A lot of their work was ecclesiastical commissions such as altar

Unfinished sample of Leek embroidery

1879

8½x 8½in (22 x 22cm)

This sample clearly shows the brown outline that was printed on the tussah silk. The leaves are worked in long and short stitch and the buds in close rows of stem stitch. The wide stem is worked in Roumanian stitch.

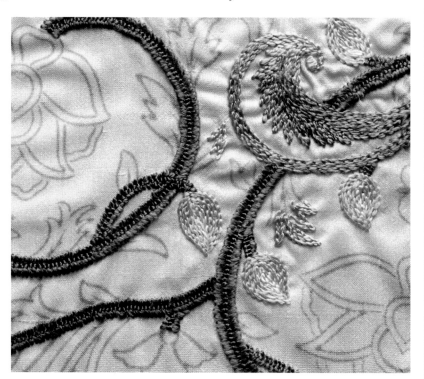

The unfinished sample of Leek embroidery.

A border of Leek embroidery

1890
4¾in (12cm) wide

An Indian-style border worked on tussah silk and possibly an Elizabeth Wardle design. The long and short stitch flowers are outlined with couched Japanese gold thread. The edge of the border has four strands of green silk thread couched down with upright yellow stitches.

An Indian-style border of Leek embroidery.

frontals and pulpit falls. Elizabeth was already an expert needlewoman in designing and producing church embroidery. There were also domestic items like cushion covers, chair backs, curtain borders and mantel trims.

The Leek School gained recognition at major exhibitions for the excellence of its work and did much to raise the status of embroidery from a leisure activity to an art form. The school premises were next to the Wardles' home and pupils were charged one guinea per lesson. It was stipulated that the students had to be of 'gentle birth'.

The Leek Embroidery Society was founded in 1879. It undertook work designed by William Morris, Walter Crane and, naturally, by Elizabeth herself. The Society also prepared 'kits' with fabric pre-printed with the design and all the threads needed to complete the project. Sometimes the kits were already started to give the recipient an idea of which stitches to use. The Wardles' London shop, in New Bond Street, was very popular.

A sample of Leek embroidery

1880

3½in (8.5cm) wide

This lovely design shows a great variety of stitches. Along the top edge there are buttonhole wheels bordered with couched gold thread. The swirling leaves are worked in long and short and the centre of the flower shape has a form of lattice couching. The opposite border has little semi-circular shapes worked in satin stitch. Unfortunately, the piece has been washed in the past. Although the coloured silk threads are perfectly fast, the core of the gold thread has run, leaving a red dye all over the tussah silk background.

A sample of Leek embroidery, 1880.

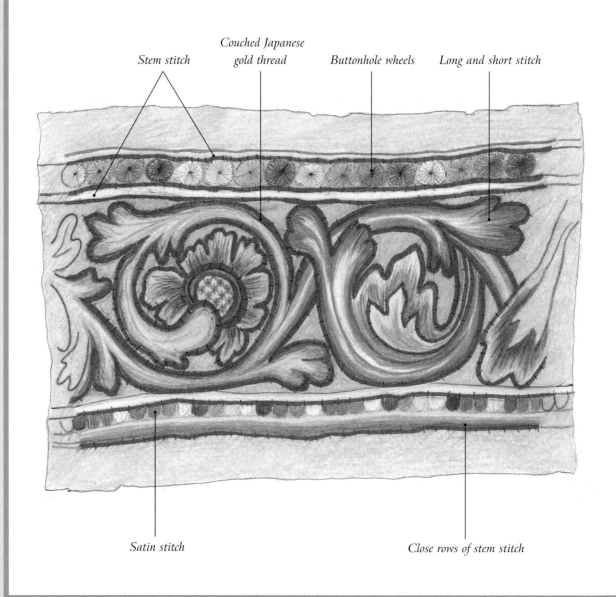

Stem stitch

Couched Japanese gold thread

Buttonhole wheels

Long and short stitch

Satin stitch

Close rows of stem stitch

Couching

Couching is a method used to apply a thread that is too thick or stiff to pass through the fabric, such as the Japanese gold used in Leek work. The couched thread is manipulated along the drawn line and held in place with little straight stitches that can be invisible or contrast depending on the design. Any form of couching is easier to work if the embroidery is mounted in a frame. Japanese gold thread had a core of fine red or orange silk. Gold leaf was applied to paper and cut into narrow strips. The gold paper was carefully spiralled around the silk thread to cover it entirely but retain its flexibility. It was available in Britain from about 1860. It was used extensively for church embroidery.

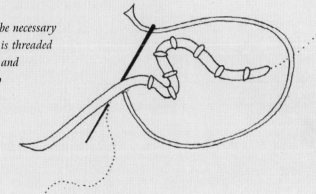

To bring the gold thread to the surface of the fabric it may be necessary to pierce a hole with a stiletto. Then a large chenille needle is threaded with a short length of fine, strong thread, which is doubled and knotted to make a small loop. The needle is pushed down to the back of the work through the hole and the end of the gold thread is passed through the loop. A quick tug on the needle and the end of the gold thread is pulled to the underside.

Roumanian stitch

Used as a filling for stems or leaves and petals.

*Bring the thread up at A and take a stitch to the middle of the motif **B–C**. Pull through keeping the thread below the needle. Make the next stitch **D–E** to hold the long stitch in place. Repeat keeping all the stitches close together to make a solid filling.*

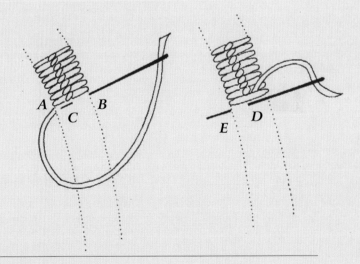

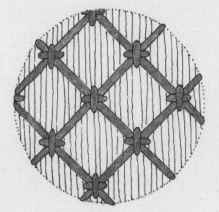

Lattice couching

First long stitches are made side by side to fill the area. Next, in a different colour, long stitches are made diagonally across the filling stitches.

At each intersection, a little cross stitch is made to hold everything in place.

Whitework

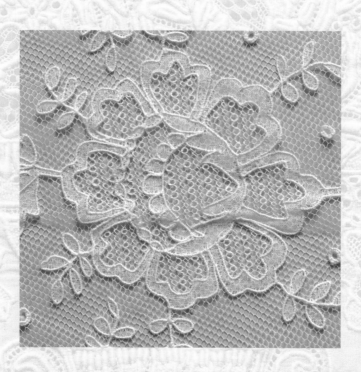

'...But embroidery on muslin is now so intimately connected
with the preparation of elegant dresses, that it appears not
only advisable, but desirable, that all ladies who are desirous
of preparing their own, should become acquainted both with its
general principles, and with a considerable portion of its
interesting details. The art, or rather this particular branch of
it, is employed most frequently in the working of flowers, either
singly or in groups; and other ornamental designs for the
borders of dresses (and in some cases, of entire ones) and also
for handkerchiefs, caps, capes, collars, and other muslin
articles of use or ornament.'

THE LADIES' HANDBOOK OF EMBROIDERY
ON MUSLIN AND LACE WORK, 1843

W HITEWORK offered a complete contrast to the embroidery activities of the 19th century lady of leisure. Victorian ladies wore white embroidered accessories and were enthusiastic followers of the latest fashions. However, these items were produced by working-class women, who were very often on the poverty line, as a supplement to the meagre family income. This came at a time when the financial differences between the poor and the middle and upper classes were at their most obvious and it is interesting to note how the humble needle became the means to provide food on the table.

Whitework designs, Indian ink on stiff white paper, mid-19th century.

'This kind of work must of course be done by a pattern; and very beautiful ones may be purchased at a moderate cost...In drawing patterns it is best to trace them first with a black lead pencil, and then to retrace them, when perfected, with Indian ink. It is easy to take a pattern from one previously worked (if on thick muslin) by laying a piece of white paper over it, and rubbing it with a nutmeg, one side of which has been rendered smooth by grating.'

EMBROIDERY ON MUSLIN, 1843

Ayrshire work

'Lessons in design learned, perhaps from snow crystals and frozen window panes; delicate traceries which told tales of an imaginative sentiment, the more lovely because those who made them hid much of their thoughts, as Scotswomen will, under a seeming hard exterior. But by their work ye shall know them; and truly these Ayrshire embroideries rank perhaps higher, technically speaking, than any needlework that the world has yet produced.'

Ann Macbeth, The Glasgow School of Art, Chief Instructress,
THE ART OF AYRSHIRE WHITE NEEDLEWORK, James A Morris, 1916

Ayrshire work was the most popular form of whitework embroidery from 1825 to the mid-1860s. Women's fashions had changed dramatically from the limp Regency-style robes to a garment with more structure and width. Wide 'gigot' sleeves and the lowered fitted waistline demanded more substantial muslin accessories such as the shoulder-wide collars called 'pelerines'.

The origins of Ayrshire work seem to come from a few directions. There is the much repeated story of a certain Mrs Jamieson of Ayr, who borrowed a French baby robe from a young widow and her child returning from Sicily in 1814. So intrigued by the embroidery and stitching, Mrs Jamieson copied the techniques and in particular the needlepoint fillings. She then taught this new form of needlework to her employees in her embroidery workshop, which originally produced tambour whitework. By the early 1820s, Mrs Jamieson was producing all manner of ladies' accessories and baby clothes. She was said to have 1,000 women in her employ and eventually passed the business on to her daughters.

However, it cannot be ignored that at the same time as Mrs Jamieson was encouraging the production of Ayrshire work in Scotland, other beautiful examples of whitework had already been imported from India. The Indian whitework or 'Chikan embroidery' can be distinguished from other forms of whitework by the contrast of heavy cotton satin stitch motifs set against the most delicate pulled work fillings. In fact, by the 1830s and 1840s, Ayrshire baby robes were being sent to India to be copied and the embroidered cloth was exported back to Europe to be made into garments.

Glasgow, Scotland and Lancashire in England were already producing fine muslin fabrics. The weaving technology had improved at the end of the 18th century and 'British mull muslin' could compete with the finest that India could produce.

Thus the combination of French, Indian and Scottish influences combined to produce a thriving industry that employed over 30,000 outworkers in Western Scotland and eventually more embroiderers in Northern Ireland. Scottish Ayrshire work displayed a stand at the Great Exhibition in 1851 in London. Following the success of this publicity, a Glasgow company in Scotland employed 2,000 men and women in their warehouses and 20,000 women home-workers to feed this demanding fashion.

Ayrshire whitework pelerine, 1835–1837.

Ayrshire whitework pelerine
1835–1837

Large collars such as this were very fashionable worn over the puffed 'gigot' sleeves. The design on the main part of the pelerine shows the pulled work centres of the large daisy flowers. The detail of the flounce shows more pulled work centres and a dainty, scalloped buttonhole edging.

Detail drawings of the Ayrshire pelerine.

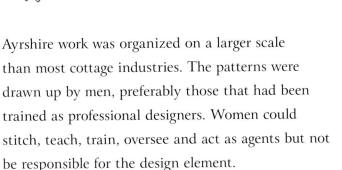

Ayrshire work was organized on a larger scale than most cottage industries. The patterns were drawn up by men, preferably those that had been trained as professional designers. Women could stitch, teach, train, oversee and act as agents but not be responsible for the design element.

At first the designs were drawn on strong paper. The muslin was placed over this and the design traced through. Then as production increased, the designs were printed with wooden blocks or rollers using water-soluble ink. Later, as the industry grew still further, the designs were lithographed directly on to the fabric, together with instructions as to how long the work should take to complete and the payment allowed. Earnings from Ayrshire work were incredibly low as with most other piece work and cottage industries.

The printed muslins and cotton threads were distributed to the out-workers by the agents. The embroiderers, or 'flowerers' as they were known, worked in their own homes. Some agents operated the 'Truck System' of payment, which offered half the wage as money and the other half as credit at the local grocery store. The store was probably owned by the agent as well. Children could earn up to a penny per week by threading needles.

'A servant in our employment many years ago, mentioned at the time, that her mother had been an embroidery worker, and that she as a girl, got on a Saturday a half-penny for threading her mother's needles and laying them in rows, in order that no time whatever might be taken from the work.'

THE ART OF AYRSHIRE WHITE NEEDLEWORK, James A Morris, 1916

As demand for Ayrshire embroidered items grew, the work spread across to Northern Ireland and even to the Island of Madeira, where it was used as relief work when the wine crop failed in 1858. Madeira work can be identified by its use of a pale blue-tinted thread.

At first, the embroiderers were responsible for completing the whole of the item assigned to them, but eventually to speed up production the pieces passed through many hands. Thus one worker would specialize in buttonhole edgings and another in intricate needlepoint fillings. The pay would reflect the standard of skill required.

The agents would then collect the finished embroideries and return them to the warehouses. Here they were laundered, ironed and wrapped in tissue paper and carefully boxed. Then they were distributed to the high street stores or sent abroad to America, Russia and France. The prices of the finished garments were very high and reflected the hours of work spent on them. Of course, the price tickets in the shops did not equate to the meagre pay received by the flowerers.

Ayrshire work was found on lady's accessories such as pelerines, collars, cuffs, chemisettes, tuckers, bonnet frills, caps and underwear. Bands, ruffles, frills and insertions were sold as lengths.

The most popular garment for Ayrshire work was the baby robe. The baby robes followed the ladies' fashion of the 1830s, with an inverted triangle for the bodice front, puffed, off the shoulder sleeves and a triangular insert in the skirt front flanked by decorative strips called 'robings'. The baby robe fastened up the centre back with ties at the neck and waist. Traditionally the bodice front had its point exposed at the waist seam for a boy and tucked in for a girl. Baby's caps had a circular crown worked in Ayrshire embroidery and these could be purchased separately so that the actual bonnet could be made up at home.

Ayrshire work declined in popularity in the 1860s when fashions changed again, favouring heavy silks and taffetas over cottons and muslins. This also coincided with the American Civil War (1861–1865), which cut off the supply of raw cotton for the muslin-weaving industry. By this time, embroidery machines were in full production and could copy whitework embroidery for the fraction of the effort and price of the handmade versions. Many of the older flowerers turned their hand to producing the coarser 'Broderie Anglais' style of whitework.

Long baby robe

1869, length from neck to hem 43in (109cm)

HERE is a beautiful example of an Ayrshire baby robe heavily embroidered on the bodice and skirt flanked by double 'robings'. The tab on the waistband shows it was intended for a boy. The detail shows the elaborate needlepoint fillings on the vase and flowers motif. The gown is entirely hand sewn with narrow French seams and fastens at the centre back with two cloth buttons and drawstrings at the neck and waist.

Baby's cap

mid-19th century

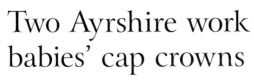

THIS cap shows Ayrshire work on the crown and the brim and displays a variety of fine needlepoint fillings. The cap is made in seven sections, which are sewn together with a faggot stitch. The brim has corded pintucks so that the drawstrings can be pulled up to fit the baby's head.

Mid-19th century baby's cap.

Two Ayrshire work babies' cap crowns

THE stitches used in both these cap crowns are padded satin, close buttonhole, stem, double back stitch and detached buttonhole.

This crown is embroidered on one piece of muslin and each needlepoint filling is a different design. Diameter 3in (7.2cm), 1830s.

This crown has the outer trim sewn to the centre medallion. Diameter 2¾in (7cm), 1830–1860.

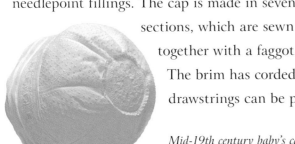

Materials and equipment

T HE supplies needed for Ayrshire work were minimal. The agents provided the muslin, ready printed with the design, and the cotton thread. A round or crewel needle, scissors and a small stiletto for eyelets would be all that was needed for the outworker to have in her workbasket.

Ayrshire work would have to be stitched under some form of tension or the muslin would pucker around the dense areas of satin stitch. It cannot be reasonably believed that all these cottage workers would have had access to embroidery hoops or frames.

This small sample of whitework (see picture below), although not authentic Ayrshire work, gives evidence to the idea that the muslin was tacked to a piece of stiff card. This piece shows the pattern being read through the fabric, but the same method could have been employed for the printed muslin. The card would be cheap, readily available and form a means of support for the fine muslin. This method of support had been used extensively in the production of needlepoint laces for centuries.

'In order to secure accuracy, the muslin is to be tacked down to the pattern, and the design must be accurately traced by running all the external edges round with cotton. It is impossible to pay too great attention to this direction, as so much of the beauty of the work depends on it.'
EMBROIDERY ON MUSLIN, 1843

Practice piece of 19th century whitework on card.

Ayrshire work stitches

THE satin stitch motifs and borders were worked first and then the muslin could be cut away in the spaces required for the needlepoint fillings. Traditionally, each needlepoint filling had to be different but all are based on a simple detached buttonhole stitch either worked horizontally or in the round. The card mount would form a good foundation as it would keep the fabric in perfect shape and could be rolled away from the needle to help make the delicate stitches.

The stitches used are mainly satin, padded satin, eyelets, close buttonhole, stem and back stitch. Feather stitch and French knots were used to decorate the seams of the garment, particularly on baby robes. All the stitches were comparatively easy to work but difficult to keep even and precise on such a small scale. Ayrshire work was a very intense form of needlework and many women suffered from bad eyesight trying to work by candlelight, for hours on end, in a dark cottages. The designs were mainly floral with stylized flowers and leaves. Scrolls, geometric and abstract shapes surround the cut-away areas.

Padded satin stitch for small motifs

1   Fill the shape with a few vertical stitches.

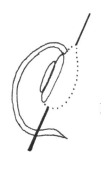

2   Cover the padding with closely worked diagonal stitches, keeping the edges exactly on the drawn shape.

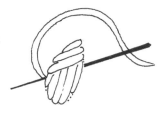

1

2

Very small eyelets

1   Pierce the muslin with a stiletto without cutting the threads of the fabric.

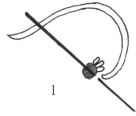

2   Work tiny over stitches by placing the needle through the hole and out just into the fabric.

1

2

Close buttonhole stitch as an edging

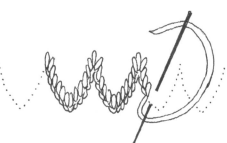

Following the drawn line, work a very narrow and close buttonhole stitch. The muslin is cut to shape after the stitching is worked.

Double back stitch

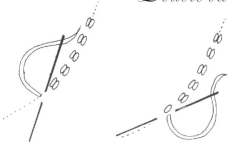

This is worked the same way as normal back stitch but the movement is repeated and a tiny gap is left between each pair of stitches

Feather stitch

1   Start by bringing the needle up at *A*. Make stitch *B–C,* putting the thread under the needle. Pull through.

2   Make stitch *D–E*, again putting the thread under the needle.

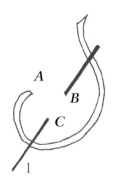
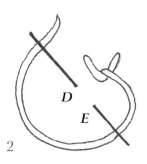
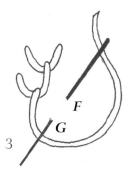

3   Repeat the same movement, *F–G*.

4   Repeat stages *2* and *3*. The feather shape can be varied but on Ayrshire work it is small and neat.

The basic needlepoint stitch

With the needle pointing upright and with the tip through the hole. Take the thread from the eye of the needle, pass it under the needle from right to left and then over the needle and pull through gently. This results in a detached buttonhole stitch with an extra twist on the leg. By varying the length of the legs and the grouping of the stitches, many different needlepoint fillings could be created. The 'pearls' were added as required.

Needlepoint fillings

The 'pearls' are the minute rings found in the needlepoint fillings and are typical of the finest quality Ayrshire work.

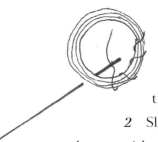

1 Wrap the thread about four times around a large darning needle and whip the threads into a small ring.

2 Slide the ring off the large needle and cover with close buttonhole stitch.

Detail of a handkerchief

mid-19th century

The three hem motifs are less than 2in (5cm) wide.

THIS handkerchief has three borders of fine Ayrshire work and shows how the needlepoint fillings were constructed using detached buttonhole stitch. The tiny ornamental rings were known as 'pearls'.

*Handkerchief showing
needlepoint fillings.*

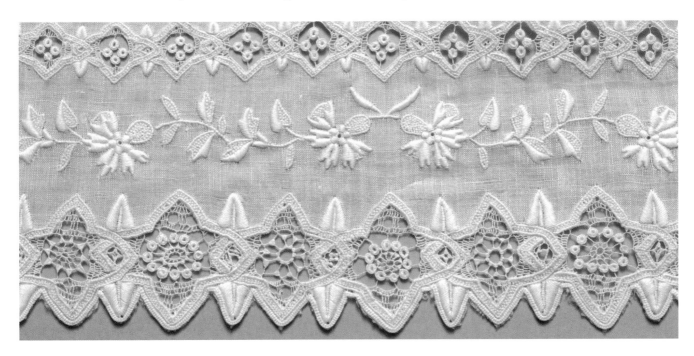

Early 19th century whitework

Long baby robe

circa 1820–1825

Length from neck to hem 43in (109cm)

The style of the robe is like the adult fashion of the time with a low neckline and a high waist. The short tight sleeves have raglan armhole seams. The unusual wide robings faced inwards and fasten at the centre front with a button. The robe fastens at the centre back with two buttons and a drawstring.

The bodice embroidery has lines of little satin stitch leaves on a running stitch stem. In between there is a double line of drawn thread work. Four fabric threads have been withdrawn from the fabric and a simple hem stitch worked, clustering four fabric threads together. To create the zigzag effect, the alternate four threads are clustered on the opposite side.

The robings and the hem of the skirt are decorated with multiple rows of pintucks stitched with running stitch. The buttons are made by gathering a circle of fabric around a small metal ring. The edge of the button is stab stitched and a star motif is worked in the centre and sleeve bindings are decorated with French knots.

This exquisite baby robe was made and worn around the time Ayrshire work was just being developed.

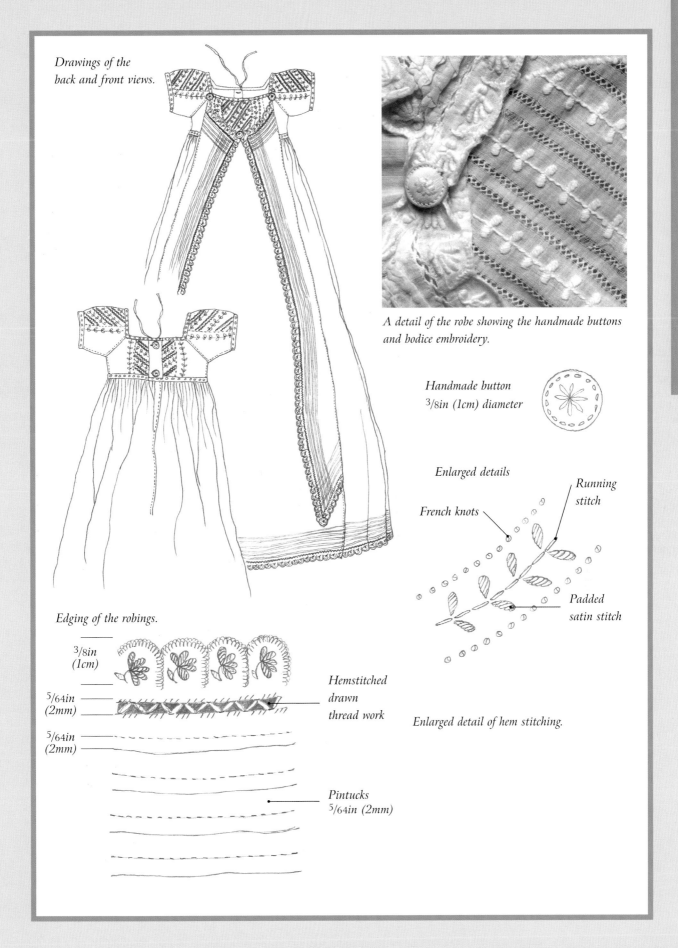

Drawings of the back and front views.

A detail of the robe showing the handmade buttons and bodice embroidery.

Handmade button
³/₈in (1cm) diameter

Enlarged details

French knots

Running stitch

Padded satin stitch

Edging of the robings.

³/₈in (1cm)

⁵/₆₄in (2mm)

⁵/₆₄in (2mm)

Hemstitched drawn thread work

Enlarged detail of hem stitching.

Pintucks
⁵/₆₄in (2mm)

Mountmellick work

'Mountmellick work will repay all the time and labour expended on it, as it is rich and effective in appearance, not difficult of execution when once the stitches are mastered, and moreover possesses the great merit of washing over and over again and remaining good to the last.'

WELDON'S PRACTICAL GUIDE TO FANCY WORK, 1885

Mountmellick, a small town near Waterford, Ireland, was founded by Quakers in the 17th century. By the 18th century, it was a thriving industrial town with cotton thread and fabric manufacturers, tanneries and an iron foundry. It was often referred to as the 'Manchester of Ireland' as its cotton goods were so renowned. However, in the early 19th century there was a decline in the manufacturing activities and this left much of the population without work or income.

In the 1820s Mrs Johanna Carter, a member of the Quaker movement, decided to help local people through their difficult times by providing work for 'local distressed gentlewomen'. She introduced a type of embroidery that used cheap and readily available materials, that is the white cotton fabric and thread. Mrs Carter developed Montmellick work as a cottage industry so that the women could work in their homes. The stitches and techniques were easy to learn and required no expensive equipment or tools.

Mrs Carter's designs were taken from the countryside. The stitches she chose emulated the texture of flowers, leaves, berries and grasses. Organizing her plant drawings into naturalistic sprays and arrangements, she drew the designs on to a white sateen cotton cloth. The stitching was worked in a matt white knitting cotton, which complemented the slight sheen of the fabric beautifully. The stitches were large and the items could be worked quite quickly. They could also be laundered easily being entirely made of cotton. A speciality of Mountmellick work was the addition of knitted, fringed borders.

Mountmellick work was shown at the major exhibitions such as the Great Exhibition in London, 1851, and the Irish Industrial Exhibition in Dublin, 1853. It was extremely popular and typical items on sale were household goods such as bed coverlets, sheets, pillow shams and table linen or personal items such as nightdress cases, brush and comb bags and dressing table or 'toilet' sets. Often the embroidery would incorporate a monogram or sets of initials.

Although the fashion for Montmellick work waned a little by the 1870s it revived in the 1880s. Ladies could purchase the white fabric ready traced with typical flower designs and they could embroider their own Mountmellick pieces. Weldon's Practical Needlework magazine published monthly volumes entirely devoted to the art of Mountmellick work. At around the same time, the 'Industrial Association' in Mountmellick was formed to provide a livelihood for women in hard times. Thus the taste for this form of needlework continued till the end of the century.

'Mountmellick work takes its name from a convent in Mountmellick, Ireland, where it originated, and it is still carried on extensively in that neighbourhood under the auspices of the Industrial Association who make a speciality of Mountmellick embroidery in its modern form, with the object of assisting distressed Irish ladies and others by the sale of work. The committee of this Association had the honour of presenting a beautifully worked toilet cover to the Princess of Wales on the occasion of Her Royal Highnesses' visit to Ireland in 1885.'

WELDON'S PRACTICAL GUIDE TO FANCY WORK, 1885

Two typical Mountmellick designs of plants of the countryside.

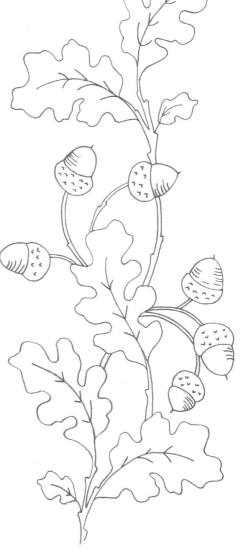

The Irish potato famine started in 1845 when the potato blight attacked the staple crop of Ireland. Approximately one third of the crop was lost. By 1846, only a quarter of the potato harvest was edible. Although the situation improved slightly in 1847, many had to resort to eating their seed potato stock. Consequently there was little left to plant. By 1848, potato crops were back to half their normal yield and by 1850 the worst effects were over.

During this terrible time, small farmers with more than 20 acres could possibly survive but peasants, with only a meagre strip of land, faced starvation. The potato was the staple food of the Irish country dweller and normally it was a reliable and low-maintenance crop. These desperate five years devastated whole families and many were turned out of their homes due to lack of work and income.

Relief came from a few directions. Some folk emigrated to Canada or America to find a better life. There were schemes for public works and road building but, apart from bringing little financial reward, this work separated families for weeks at a time. Well-meaning ladies sought to set up needlework and craft employment for the women and girls with the hope that it would provide a small helpful income. From these attempts to provide useful and profitable occupations came a few of our most delightful forms of embroidery.

A small dressing table mat
mid-19th century

BLACKBERRIES worked in French knots and satin stitch dog roses decorate this small mat. The leaves are worked in Bokhara couching. The mat is bordered by the typical Mountmellick knitted fringe.

Small Mountmellick work table mat.

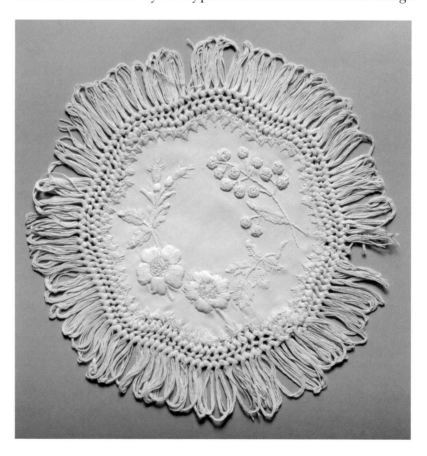

Materials and equipment

The white cotton fabric that was already manufactured in Mountmellick was called 'jean'. It was cotton sateen and had a slight sheen. The thread was loosely twisted cotton knitting yarn and was pure matt white. The result of this match of the shiny fabric with the matt thread was a particular characteristic of Mountmellick work.

Weldon's Practical Guide recommended 'Strutts' knitting cotton, number 8 or 10 being a suitable weight for the embroidery and number 6 for padding. A crewel needle was used with an eye large enough to accommodate the thread. A thimble would have been useful for some stitches, such as bullion knots.

There was no need for a frame to stretch the fabric as the stitches were worked over the finger and the fabric held in the hand. The jean fabric, coming straight from the loom, would have been quite stiff and thus held its shape. The fabric would then soften when the completed item was washed.

Knitting needles were required for knitted fringes. Using four balls of number 12 knitting cotton, four strands were knitted together on a pair of number 11 (3mm) knitting needles (see box below for instructions).

'For toilet covers or mats, bedspreads and such articles, Mountmellick work is without equal for beauty of design and durability.'
WELDON'S PRACTICAL MOUNTMELLICK EMBROIDERY, 1885

The knitted fringe

- Using 4 strands of number 12 knitting cotton and number 11 needles, cast on 12 stitches.
- *Make 1 (by making a yarn over), knit 2 together, knit 1*, repeat * to * 3 times.
- Every row is the same.
- Knit sufficient length and cast off 7 stitches, break yarn and draw the end through the last cast-off stitch on the right-hand needle.
- Slip the remaining 5 stitches off the left-hand needle and unravel these back to the beginning to produce a lovely fringe. This may be steamed to remove the crinkles if desired.

Adapted from Weldon's Practical Mountmellick Embroidery, *1885*

Tablecloth with a knitted fringe

late 19th century

23½ x 31½ in (60 x 80cm)

Detail of the tablecloth.

THIS detail shows honeysuckle flowers. Here the Mountmellick stitch and cable plait are used for the stems of the flowers. The scalloped edge is stitched with a close buttonhole, which also features a small scallop.

A brush and comb bag

mid-19th century

Length, including the fringe, 15¼in (39cm)

Mid-19th century brush and comb bag.

MOUNTMELLICK work showing a bunch of summer flowers using the following stitches: buttonhole, stem, satin, bullion knots and feather. 'Toilet' bags, such as this one, were popular Mountmellick work items.

Pillow sham

circa 1870

Detail drawing of a pillow sham stitched in Mountmellick work showing how the various stitches are used to suggest the textures of the flowers, leaves, berries and wheatears.

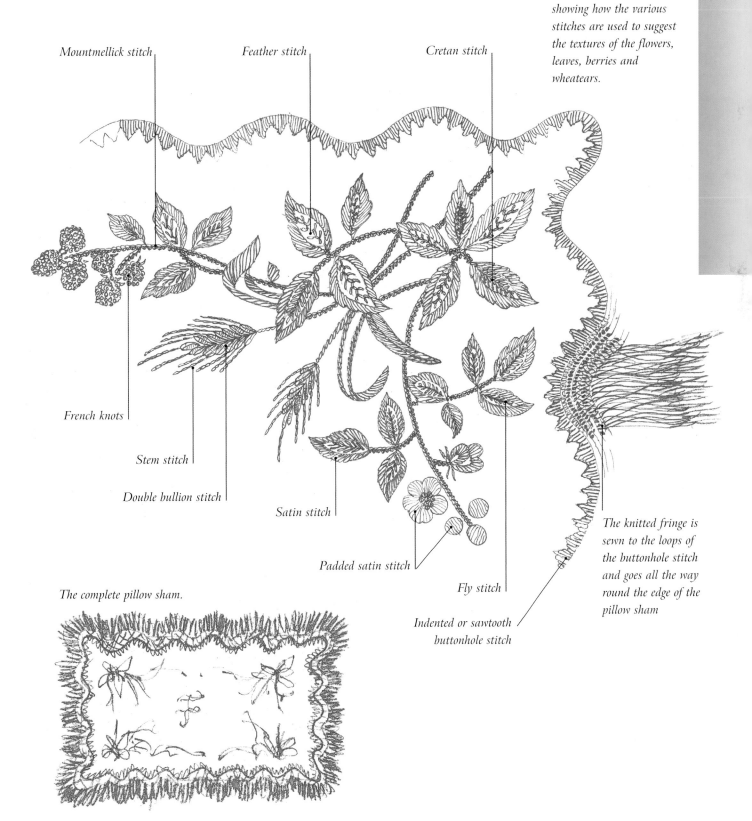

Mountmellick stitch

Feather stitch

Cretan stitch

French knots

Stem stitch

Double bullion stitch

Satin stitch

Padded satin stitch

Fly stitch

Indented or sawtooth buttonhole stitch

The knitted fringe is sewn to the loops of the buttonhole stitch and goes all the way round the edge of the pillow sham

The complete pillow sham.

Mountmellick stitch

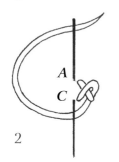

1

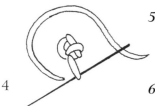

2

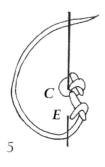

3

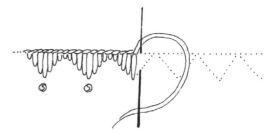

4

5

Mountmellick work stitches

Although Mountmellick work had a huge repertoire of stitches, most of them are the basic stem, back, chain and satin stitch. However, there were some more uncommon stitches that were used to imitate the texture of the flowers and leaves.

Mountmellick stitch

1   Start by bringing the needle up at *A* and make stitch *C–B*. Pass the needle under this stitch without going through the fabric.

2   Make stitch *A–C,* putting the thread under the needle point, and pull through.

3   Make stitch *E–D* and pull through.

4   Pass the needle under this stitch without going through the fabric.

5   Make the stitch *C–E*, going through the chain loop at *C* and putting the thread under the needlepoint, pull through.

6   Repeat stages *3*, *4* and *5*.

Sawtooth or indented buttonhole edging

Work buttonhole stitch in the normal way following a line to keep the sawtooth effect even. Sometimes French knots are worked at the points.

6

Cable plait stitch

1 Bring the needle up at *A* and twist the thread around the tip by putting the needle und er the thread, then the thread over the needle. Hold in place with the left thumb.

2 Twist the needle backwards and insert at *B* and come up at *C*, taking the thread under the needle point, and pull through.

3 Repeat this last movement.

Cable plait stitch

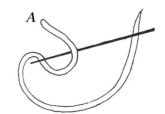

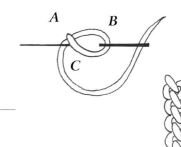

Fly stitch

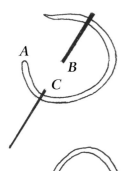

Fly stitch

1 Bring the needle up at *A*. Make stitch *B–C*, putting the thread under the needle point, and pull through.

2 Insert the needle at *D* to make a holding stitch.

3 Repeat these two movements. Fly stitch can be used in a line or individually as a filling stitch.

Bokhara couching

Bokhara couching

1 Bring the needle up at *A*. Take a long stitch across the shape to be filled and make stitch *B–C*, pull through.

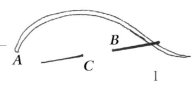

2 Make stitch *D–E* and pull through. *D–E* makes a little couching stitch that holds down the long stitch.

3 Space the couching stitches in a regular pattern.

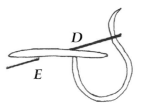

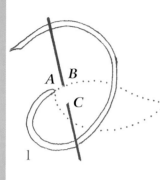

Cretan stitch

1   Bring the needle up at **A**. Make the stitch **B–C**, putting the thread under the needle point. Pull through.

2   Make stitch **D–E**, again putting the thread under the needle point.

3   Move to the initial side and repeat stitch, **F–G**.

4   Repeat the movement working from side to side of the shape.

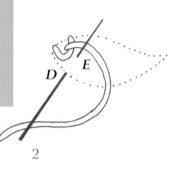

Bullion stitch

Bullion stitch

1   Bring the needle up at **A**.
Take stitch **B–A** but do not pull the needle completely through.

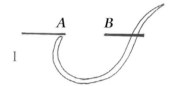

2   Wrap the needle 4–6 times clockwise. The number of twists depends on the length of **A–B**.

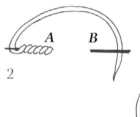

3   Keep the thumb on the twists, relaxing the tension of the twists slightly, and carefully pull the needle through. Take the needle back down at **B**.

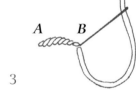

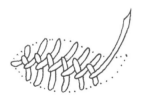

Double bullion stitch

Double bullion stitches are worked to represent wheat ears in Mountmellick work.

Double bullion stitch

Carrickmacross work

Although defined as an Irish lace, Carrickmacross was really an embroidered net. Around the year 1820, Mrs Grey Porter, who lived in Donaghmoyne, not far from the town of Carrickmacross, acquired a piece of lace from Italy. Intrigued by the embroidery, she taught her sewing maid, Mary Steadman, how to copy the technique. The lace was much admired and Mary received orders for more pieces from the local gentry.

Later, Miss Reid of Rahans, also near Carrickmacross, came to explore this lace embroidery and taught her sister how to work the technique. They soon conceived the idea of teaching local women how to work the lace, to help them earn some form of livelihood. In a short time they had converted an outhouse on their brother's farm into a Lace School and they began to teach young girls the art of Carrickmacross lace work.

This technique began before the famine troubles but was sustained during and after the potato blight as a regular means of income for dextrous women and girls. Although many such schools were set up in Ireland, Carrickmacross remained the centre for supplying designs and organizing orders.

Carrickmacross was used for all forms of ladies' accessories such as collars, cuffs, stoles, bonnets and caps, fans and parasol covers, flounces and dress trims, indeed any garment that a fine lace would enhance. However, the construction was not robust enough for children's clothes.

Carrickmacross used floral or abstract curvilinear designs, often including shamrocks. The edges were usually scalloped and finished with picots. A feature is the complex needle darned fillings found on the net areas. The work is carried out in white or cream and darker examples have usually been dyed with tea or coffee.

A young lady of 1838 wearing a bonnet flounce and pelerine of Carrickmacross lace.

Detail of the bonnet flounce, length 71¼in (181cm) and width 8in (20cm).

It is pinned to the bonnet brim under silk ribbon bows.

Method of working

The design is drawn on a stiff, glazed cotton cloth, which was flexible enough to curve in the hand when stitching. On to this cloth was laid a layer of machine net and on top of this a layer of fine muslin. All were smoothed out and tacked in place, the tacking stitches going around the motifs, not over them. The design would be clearly seen through the fabrics.

A linen or cotton thread was couched with a finer thread along all the outlines of the design. The tiny stitches were worked through the muslin and net but not through the glazed cotton. In old instructions the couching was often called 'whipping'. The best quality work had the couching stitches worked very closely together forming a raised, corded effect, hence the other description, also much used, of 'cording'. All the outlines needed to be a continuous line to avoid constantly cutting the cording thread. This was one of the features of Carrickmacross, and where necessary the thread doubled back and the twin outline was couched as one. Precision was required to make corners sharp and curves smooth.

The outside edge was decorated with picots made by twisting the thread into a little loop and catching in place with one or two stitches. A pin could be used to regulate the size of the picots but it was usually done by eye.

On completion of all the outlines, edges and eyelets or spots, the tacking stitches were cut from the back of the glazed cotton and the work released. The pattern could be re-used several times over. The fabric was held over the hand and using appliqué scissors, with one bulbous blunt blade, the muslin was cut away from the background areas leaving the motifs floating on a net ground.

The next stage was to work the centres of flowers with needle darning fillings. These were worked with a very fine thread. As the front and back of the stitches could be seen through the net, simple cross stitches appeared like complicated lace embroidery.

This type of embroidery was known as 'Carrickmacross appliqué'. Another version was known as 'Carrickmacross guipure', which had no net background. The motifs were connected by buttonhole bridges or 'brides', which were worked before the muslin was removed from the glazed cotton pattern. Often the brides were enhanced with straight picots or 'thorns' worked in buttonhole stitch. A combination of the two techniques was very attractive.

An advertisement for threads for Carrickmacross work and other Irish laces from The Home Art of Fancy Stitchery, *edited by Flora Klickman.*

Unfortunately Carrickmacross lace was very difficult to launder. The muslin tended to shrink and pull away from the net. The best method was to wash gently by hand, rinse and place the wet lace on a sheet of glass or a mirror and then ease into shape. When dry, the lace required no ironing and the couched lines were not flattened.

' "Yes", said that lady, "such lace cannot be got now for love or money; Made by the nuns abroad they tell me...Of course your ladyship knows that such lace must never be starched or ironed. Some people wash it in sugar and water; and some in coffee, to make it the right yellow colour; but I myself have a very good receipt for washing it in milk, which stiffens it enough, and gives it a very good creamy colour." '
CRANFORD, Mrs Gaskell, 1853

Cornucopia, height 5in (12.5cm). A very fine and detailed piece of Carrickmacross, possibly a sample worked by a student.

Materials and equipment

The designs were hand drawn on to the glazed cotton or cambric with Indian ink. This often penetrated to the back of the cloth so the pattern could be flipped for a mirror image. Thus, only half a collar pattern was required. Paper or thin card was often used as a substitute. Later on in the century, the patterns could be purchased ready printed and drawn by professional Carrickmacross designers.

The net was a square or diamond construction, depending on the angle it was viewed from. It was known as Carrickmacross net and was of a very fine quality. Some instructions recommend 'Brussels' net as this was available in widths of 36, 72 and 144 inches and did not require any seaming.

The muslin was closely woven and slightly transparent. The muslin used for the guipure work was slightly thicker. It was tightly woven so that it would not readily fray when cut.

A few weights of thread were needed; a thick thread for the outlining the motifs and a finer one for couching this to the fabrics. A very fine thread was used for the needle darning fillings. Crochet thread was often used, the recommended thicknesses being numbers 80 and 200.

Ordinary sewing needles were used, a sharps number 10 being the usual size. A fine blunt needle would have been useful for the needle darning but not absolutely necessary.

Historical threads

The first machine-made nets were made at the end of the 18th century. By 1809 John Heathcoat was producing a twisted hexagonal net ground, which would not unravel when cut. By the 1820s, machine-made net was readily available and the use of steam power had speeded up production. The nets were made with cotton thread and this made the purchase price very reasonable. By 1830, a new net with a diamond-shaped mesh began to replace Heathcoat's version and this was the type favoured for Carrickmacross work.

The stitches and method of working

'In whipping it will be found more satisfactory to make the stitches slanting. The whipping blends better with the couching thread, thereby rendering the stitches almost invisible.'

WELDON'S PRACTICAL CARRICKMACROSS LACE, 1885

Carrickmacross appliqué

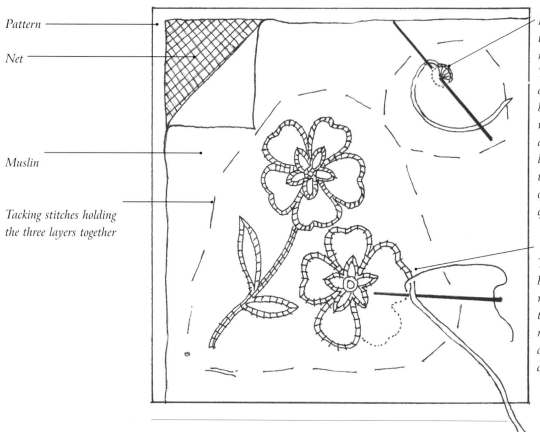

Pattern

Net

Muslin

Tacking stitches holding the three layers together

Eyelets are worked through the muslin and net. They are finished off with two tiny buttonhole stitches worked on the edge and pulled tight like a knot and the thread snipped off close to the eyelet.

The thicker thread being couched or whipped, around the outline of the motif to give the characteristic corded edge

Looping the picot edging

Working from right to left, make a loop by putting the needle-point under the cording thread. Twist the needle to the right, anti-clockwise, up then down again. Then put the point into the fabric, bringing it up a small distance along the pattern line. Regulate the size of the picot with the left thumb. Wherever possible continue the motif outline into the picot border and back out again so that it is firmly attached to the fabric.

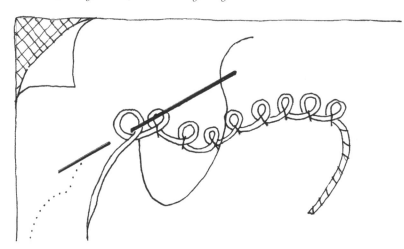

A Carrickmacross stole

1830–1840

19½ x 78¾in (50 x 200cm)

THIS is an unfinished piece of Carrickmacross at the stage when the tacking stitches have been cut and the work has been removed from the paper pattern. The embroiderer has just begun to cut away the muslin background and reveal the net. Some net darning fillings have been worked The work is very long and narrow and at the other end the net and muslin is still tacked to the paper pattern and the stitching yet to be started. The design is hand-drawn on the paper with Indian ink.

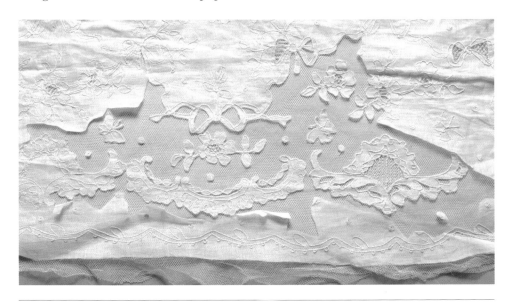

An unfinished Carrickmacross stole.

Needle darning fillings

The stitches used in needle darning the lace areas of Carrickmacross were very simple. Cross and running, darning and blanket stitch were used effectively. As the back of the stitch could be seen through the net, they appear more complicated than they actually are.

The net was of a square construction but seen on the diagonal it appears more like a diamond shape. The net had a soft structure and this helped the draping qualities of costume pieces.

A variety of needle darning fillings.

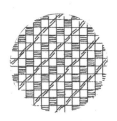
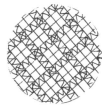
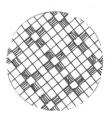
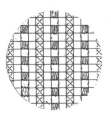
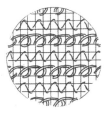
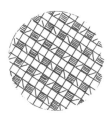

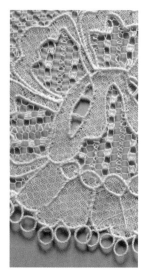

Detail showing the delicate needle darn fillings and the picot edging.

The construction of Carrickmacross guipure.

Large collar

1847

Length from neck
to centre back
10½in (27cm)

The point of the collar was worn at the back and the collar pinned at the neck with a brooch.

Carrickmacross guipure

Carrickmacross guipure has no net foundation and the motifs are held together with 'brides' or bars. As the shapes are outlined the cording thread takes a detour to join the adjacent motif by slipping under its cording and returning. This bar is covered with buttonhole stitch worked with the needle thread.

Little 'thorns' or picots are worked on alternate sides on the way back. These are made by taking a long buttonhole stitch in the muslin but only catching a couple of fabric threads. The little thorn is then covered with buttonhole stitch and the work is continued back on the main bar. When the background is cut away the thorns are released by snipping the few fabric threads that are holding them.

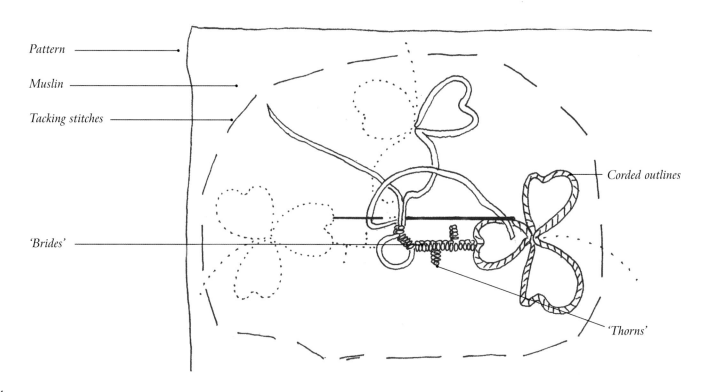

Pattern

Muslin

Tacking stitches

Corded outlines

'Brides'

'Thorns'

A narrow Carrickmacross guipure trim

1890–1900

1in (2.7cm) wide

This enlarged detail shows the brides and thorns typical of guipure work.

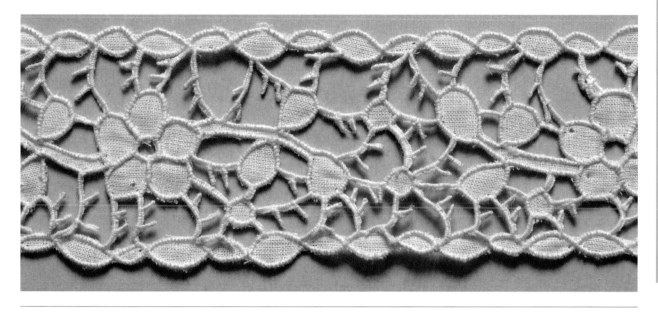

This enlarged detail shows the brides and thorns typical of guipure work.

A Bertha

1839

9½ x 53½in (24 x 136cm)

Tᴴɪs wide flounce was gathered around the neck of an off the shoulder evening dress. This style of collar was known as a 'Bertha' and was fashionable in one form or another from 1830 to 1835.

The detail shows how Carrickmacross appliqué and guipure were combined on one piece of work.

Traditional smocking

'It is made of strong linen, similar to that used for sheeting, and the biasing (sic. smocking) upon it is worked with the strongest glazed thread or cotton that can be procured. The work must be firmly and regularly done, as the price of these frocks depends on the quantity and quality of work in them.'

THE WORKWOMAN'S GUIDE, by a Lady, 1838

The smock was an outer garment worn by country workers in the 18th and 19th centuries as protective clothing. The loose style developed from men's shirts, which had gathers over the chest, back, sleeve heads and cuffs. The stitches that controlled these gathers on the smocks, became more and more decorative and the technique came to be known as 'gaging' or smocking. A feature of smocking is that although it fixes the gathers and controls the fullness of the garment, it retains a certain amount of elasticity and allows for plenty of movement.

The cut of the smock was extremely simple and made full use of the yardage of cloth. The garment was made up of rectangles and squares and could be cut using one measurement and by simply folding the fabric.

For a man, using 36in (91.5cm) wide cloth, take 4yds (3.5m) or the length from neck to hem multiplied by three. Fold the cloth into three equal lengths; two lengths make the front and back of the smock. The third piece folds into approximately three. Two parts become the sleeves. The remaining part is cut for the collar, cuffs, armhole gussets, shoulder straps and pockets.

Plan for cutting out the smock.

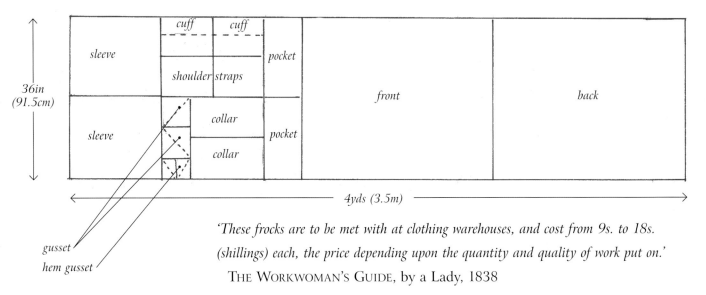

'These frocks are to be met with at clothing warehouses, and cost from 9s. to 18s. (shillings) each, the price depending upon the quantity and quality of work put on.'

THE WORKWOMAN'S GUIDE, by a Lady, 1838

Styles of smock

There are two main styles of smock. The round smock, where the front
and back were identical, and the coat smock, which buttoned down the
front. Early 19th century smocks had very little smocking, just a narrow
band controlling the gathers at the neck, shoulders and wrists. By the 1830s,
the smocks were becoming much more decorative with smocking and
embroidery covering the whole of the chest and back body. On either side
of the 'tubing' (the smocking) were 'boxes' that displayed elaborate
embroidered designs that were echoed on the collar, shoulder straps, pockets
and cuffs. The pocket could be a slit in the side seam to allow access to the
trouser pocket or a proper pocket with a flap. The shoulder straps were
often made of double cloth, as they would take the most wear from yokes
or harnesses used for ploughing.

The smock was most fashionable in the mid-19th century and was worn
not only for labouring but also for special occasions, celebrations and
outings. Most workers had two smocks, one for work and one for 'best'.

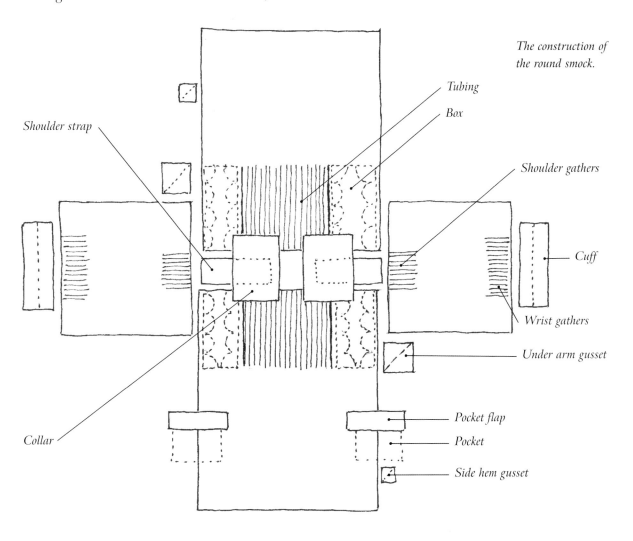

*The construction of
the round smock.*

Tubing

Box

Shoulder strap

Shoulder gathers

Cuff

Wrist gathers

Under arm gusset

Collar

Pocket flap

Pocket

Side hem gusset

Shepherds were often poor attendants at church on Sundays, due to tending their flocks away from the village. For this reason, when they died, it is said that they were buried in their smocks to prove that their profession had prevented them from regular church going. Later in the century smocks were factory made, the embroidery and smocking being outsourced to home-workers. These mass-produced smocks were of an inferior quality to the handmade smocks. By the end of the century, the decline of the smock was brought about by the increase in farm machinery. The loose smock would have been a hazard as it could so easily be caught up in mechanical moving parts. It was also considered to be old fashioned and had connotations with the 'country bumpkin' image.

Smock
circa 1814

The complete smock.

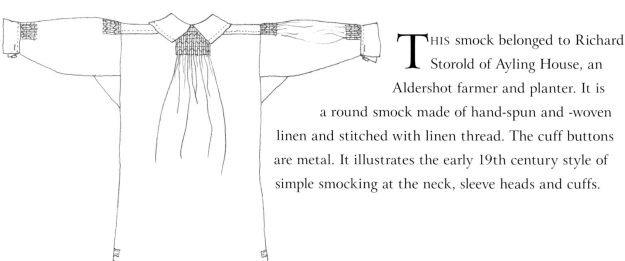

THIS smock belonged to Richard Storold of Ayling House, an Aldershot farmer and planter. It is a round smock made of hand-spun and -woven linen and stitched with linen thread. The cuff buttons are metal. It illustrates the early 19th century style of simple smocking at the neck, sleeve heads and cuffs.

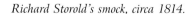

Richard Storold's smock, circa 1814.

The smocking stitches used for the 'tubing' to control the gathers.

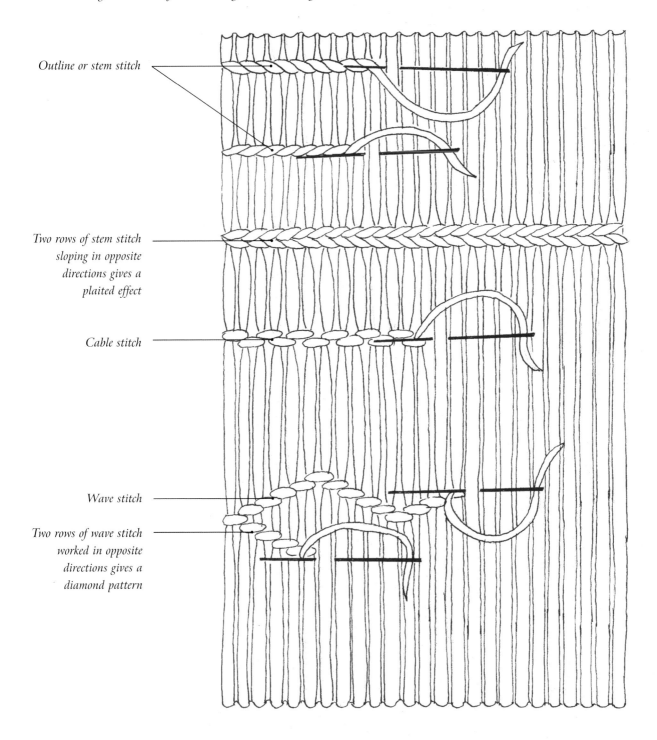

Outline or stem stitch

Two rows of stem stitch
sloping in opposite
directions gives a
plaited effect

Cable stitch

Wave stitch

Two rows of wave stitch
worked in opposite
directions gives a
diamond pattern

Broderie Anglaise

'True Broderie Anglaise patterns are outlines of various sized holes, arranged to make floral or geometrical devices.'

THE DICTIONARY OF NEEDLEWORK, SFA Caulfield & BC Saward, 1885

Broderie Anglaise became very popular for ladies' wear in the mid-19th century as it was worked on a heavier cotton fabric and could stand constant laundering and ironing. For this reason it was particularly popular for underwear, night attire, bed linen and children's clothes.

The designs are repetitive and most frequently seen as borders with scalloped edgings. The main features are the eyelets, being large or small, round or tear-drop shape, and these are linked by delicate lines and embroidered motifs.

Many of the Scottish embroiderers turned to producing Broderie Anglaise when the delicate Ayrshire embroidery ceased to be so fashionable. It was much quicker to work and did not need the eyesight and patience that the Ayrshire needlepoint fillings required. However, even low paid cottage workers could not compete with the new commercial embroidery machines that took over most of the whitework production after the 1840s.

Child's dress

1840
Length 20½in (52cm)

THE skirt and sleeves flounces have piped seams. The skirt is tightly gathered on to the waistband, which would have been covered with a ribbon sash. The neckline is finished with a narrow crochet trim.

The dress fastens at the centre back with three buttons and a tie, which pulls in the neck edge to fit the child. The waistband fastens with two hooks and eyes.

The bodice, sleeves and skirt flounce are all worked in hand-stitched Broderie Anglaise.

The detail shows the charming heart motif, which is repeated around the skirt flounce.

Materials and equipment

The fabric was a firmly woven, opaque cotton fabric usually woven in the cotton mills of the North West of England.

'Broderie Anglaise combined with satin stitch is also worked on smooth fine flannel and wincey for ladies' underwear, and for wee garments intended for the use of little people.'
WELDON'S PRACTICAL GUIDE TO FANCY WORK, 1885

The thread was a soft, mercerized cotton either softly twisted or stranded. The weight of the thread would depend on the fineness of the work.
A coarser thread than the embroidery thread was used for padding the satin stitch. A short thread length was recommended.

The patterns were available as transfers that could be ironed onto fabric or as ready-traced goods available from repositories. There were also strips of cloth ready cut or hole-punched in preparation for working the eyelets. This method would have only worked with very simple designs and is similar to the technique employed for the embroidery machines.

A crewel needle with an eye large enough to accommodate the thread was needed, together with a stiletto or piercer to make the eyelets. Sharp small scissors were required to cut the inside of the holes before working the overcasting.

Broderie Anglaise was usually worked in the hand, as it was then easier to control the overcast and buttonhole stitches. An embroidery hoop could have been used for more complex pieces of work to prevent puckering.

A strip of cotton fabric ready traced with an eyelet design 2½in (6.5cm) wide with pattern number 1396 printed on its side.

A strip of stiffened cotton fabric with punched holes and cut slits, one row of the design above the other. This is how the fabric was prepared for the Houldsworth embroidery machines and this may have been cut from such a piece.

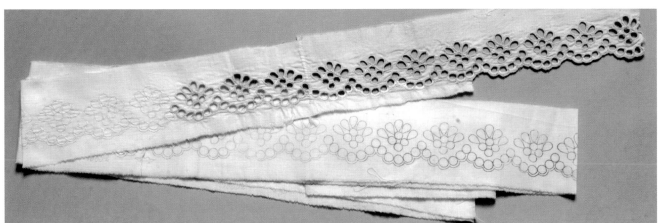

Machine Broderie Anglaise

The machine Broderie Anglaise does not have a spool thread like modern machine embroidery so is difficult to identify from handwork. However, by viewing the back of the embroidery there are a few features to look out for:

- The designs are in straight rows.
- The thread always jumps from one motif to the other at exactly the same place. This could not happen with hand embroidery even if the needle threads were pre-cut to the same length.
- The repeat is always 1½in (3.8cm) or multiples of 1½in, ie: 3in if every other needle were to be taken out of the machine.
- The edging or scallop is worked in satin stitch. Even Houldsworth's machine could not work the loop under the needle movement required for buttonhole.

A fashionable lady of 1850 wearing 'false sleeves' under the pagoda-shaped sleeves of her dress.

The detail shows the Broderie Anglaise embroidery on the cuff. The large buttonhole stitch eyelets have been filled with needle-made wheels. This style of Broderie Anglaise could not be made on a machine.

Blouse trimmings
1890–1900

A blouse front, collar and cuffs embroidered by hand, ready to be made up into a blouse. It is neatly worked combining Broderie Anglaise eyelets with whitework satin stitch flowers. The edge has a scalloped buttonhole stitch border.

Historical threads

The first commercial embroidery machines were in production by 1775 but by 1820 Josué Heilmann of Mulhouse, Germany, had refined a machine that could do the work of at least a dozen embroiderers.

The machine was quite simple in concept. The fabric was stretched in a large frame and held vertically. There were two horizontal lines of 12 pincers on either side. The needle, which had an eye in the centre, was threaded up. The pincers pushed the needle through the fabric and the pincers on the other side grabbed the needle and pushed it back through the fabric to begin again. The pincers were operated by a worker on each side and used a treadle mechanism. The frame moved up and down and side to side, so although the needles were at a fixed height, the stitches were created by the frame's movement.

The movement of the frame was created by a worker at the end of the machine using a pantograph, which traced the lines of the pattern. The pattern was drawn six times the size of the actual embroidery, so it would be easy to follow and would clearly show the path of each stitch.

A couple of workers, usually children, would run up and down each side of the machine checking for missed stitches and any needles running out of thread. The thread was used economically and cut to the exact length to complete a motif or two. Finishers were employed to darn in loose ends and replace missing stitches. These early machines were mainly used for embroidering waistcoat fabrics and dress trims.

Despite Heilmann winning awards for his invention, the embroidery machine did not really catch on and passed through various hands including being patented in England in 1829. At this time, the machines and all the rights were purchased by Mr Henry Houldsworth of Manchester, England. Houldsworth improved the pincer movement and replaced the treadle with an automatic mechanism, thus relieving a least two workers of their duties. By 1859, Houldsworth had 20 machines in continuous operation and continued to dominate the market until the mid-1870s. At this stage the machines were still producing surface embroidery. It took until 1869 for further developments that enabled the machines to embroider eyelets and holes to imitate hand-sewn Broderie Anglaise. The holes were punched in the cloth prior to stretching on the frame; by the 1870s this method was in full production for embroidering yards of trim for petticoats and baby clothes.

Petticoat flounce

circa 1850

9½in (24cm) wide

Embroidered on fine cotton this is a complex design of oval, round and pointed eyelets. All the eyelets are neatly overcast and the edge is finished with close buttonhole stitch.

Petticoat flounce

circa 1865

6¾in (17cm) wide

This flounce has a lyre-shaped design of oval eyelets that repeats along the length. The eyelets are overcast and the leaf motifs have stem stitch stems. The scalloped edge is buttonholed.

1

2

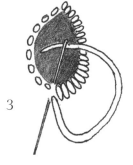

3

Broderie Anglaise stitches

'The eyelets play a leading part in Broderie Anglaise, it is essential to master these first.'

WELDON'S PRACTICAL GUIDE TO FANCY WORK, 1885

Eyelets

1 Following the lines of the design, the eyelets are first stitched round with tiny running stitches. All the shapes can be outlined with a continuous thread. There is no need to start and finish with each motif.

2 The inside of the eyelet is then cut in a cross shape and the fabric folded back to the wrong side to make the hole.

3 The eyelet is overcast, stitching through the two layers of fabric. As each eyelet is finished, any excess fabric on the back can be carefully trimmed away. Sometimes, such as when an eyelet forms the outside edge of the item, close buttonhole stitch is used. In this case the very outside edge is not cut until the embroidery is completed.

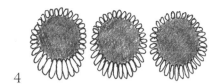 

4

5

4 The stitches can be graduated in size around the shape to give emphasis. These wider areas may be padded under the satin stitch. The padding can be stitched at the same time as the initial outlines.

5 For little eyelets, the fabric is pierced with a stiletto and the resulting hole is simply overcast.

'Do not cut away the waste linen outside the Buttonhole until the work has been washed, as it will then wear longer, and there is less fear of cutting the embroidery cotton in the process.'

THE DICTIONARY OF NEEDLEWORK, SFA Caulfield and BC Saward, 1885

Ladders

Ladders in various shapes and forms are also found in Broderie Anglaise work.

1 The shape is stitched around but when the position for the bar is reached a thread is taken across the shape picking up a little fabric, back again to the first side and back over again.

2 The three-thread bar thus formed is whipped, without the needle going through the fabric, and the outline running stitched continued to the next bar.

3 The fabric is cut behind the bars, folded back, and the motif overcast around the edges.

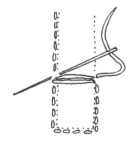 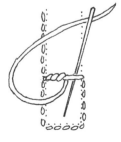 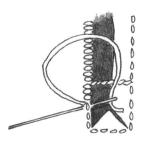

1   2   3

Patchwork and Appliqué

'In no department of ladies' fancy work has more improvement
been made of late years, than in Patchwork, and now, instead
of being a childish occupation, and only resorted to as a means
of using up scraps that would otherwise be wasted,
it has become quite a favourite work, and in its highest form
is deserving of a still more extended application, as it looks
bright and pretty in a room, and furniture covered with
it is particularly effective.'

WELDON'S PRACTICAL SHILLING GUIDE TO FANCY WORK, 1885

Throughout history and into the present day, needlewomen have been notorious for their habit of saving fabric scraps. 'Bit bags' could contain new cloth from dressmaking offcuts or bits and pieces salvaged from old clothes and furnishings. Every piece had to be saved for its rarity, thrift or sentimental value and put to a second use.

With these scraps of cloth, needlewomen have created elaborate projects that became cherished because of all the time, thought and energy that was invested into them. Many such items were bed or cot quilts that could be displayed to full advantage or were created to celebrate a special occasion. Some appliqué and patchwork pieces were started and then completed by the next generation and thus included fabrics spanning at least 50 years or more. The maxim that a quilt is only as old as its youngest fabric is a useful one to observe. Many pieces included a dedication or a date of completion to help place the item in an historical context.

'Patchwork:- This needlework, which consists in sewing pieces of material together to form a flat unbroken surface, possesses many advantages, as it is not only useful and ornamental, but forms out of odds and ends of silk, satin, or chintz, which would have been otherwise thrown away, a handsome piece of work.'

THE DICTIONARY OF NEEDLEWORK, SFA Caulfield and BC Saward, 1885

Broderie Perse

'Have you remembered to collect pieces for the Patchwork? – We are now at a standstill.'

LETTER FROM JANE AUSTEN TO HER SISTER CASSANDRA, May 1811.

Appliqué or applied work was the technique where motifs were cut out of a contrasting fabric and stitched to a new cloth ground. The type of appliqué popular in the late 18th and early 19th centuries was called 'Broderie Perse' and involved the use of the printed motifs found on chintz dress and furnishing fabrics imported from India. The fabrics were block printed with a black dye paste and usually hand-coloured on a natural cotton ground. The colours used were predominantly red, yellow, blue and green. The green areas, which were created by printing yellow dye over blue, have now faded to a dull blue.

Historical threads

In *The Workwoman's Guide* written in 1838, the author recommends that a 'rag bag is a desirable thing to have hung up in some conspicuous part of the house, into which all odd bits, and even shreds of calico, print, linen, muslin &c should be put'.

The 'Lady', which is the only name we have for this esteemed author, goes on to remark that even the smallest piece of cloth will be useful for small articles, repairs or even for practising needlework stitches.

In this day of 'throw away' textiles it is notable how previous generations treasured cloth even if it was worn or faded. It is due to their thrifty habits that many beautiful pieced and appliquéd quilts and covers have survived until today.

The motifs were cut from the cloth and placed on a plain natural-coloured ground to make an attractive scene or a floral arrangement. There was usually a complete disregard for scale of the motifs and this resulted in the charming naive quality, so characteristic of Broderie Perse.

'...the essentials of the work, that of laying one material upon another, will depend on the selection of flowers, &c. The best come from old pieces of chintz manufactured before the days of aniline dyes; their shades mix together without offence, and the outlines are generally clear and decided.'

THE DICTIONARY OF NEEDLEWORK, SFA Caulfield and BC Saward, 1885

Arabian prince on horseback
1780–1830
37½ x 43¼in (95 x 110cm)

THIS is the centre of a bedcover which is either unfinished or unpicked from a complete piece. The motifs have been cut from 18th century block prints and could date back to the 1770s and it is a very good example of Broderie Perse. The printed motifs are applied to a linen ground using slip stitches and the piece is edged with a 'Vandyke' or 'dog-tooth' border.

Arabian Prince on horseback, 1780–1830.

112

Method of working

The motifs were cut out of the scrap fabric leaving a scant ¼in (0.5cm) allowance for turning under the raw edge. They were then arranged in a pleasing manner on a cream-coloured fabric, either natural linen or cotton, that would have been previously washed and ironed. After deciding which motifs would overlap and where the ends of stems could be hidden, the whole design was tacked into place.

The motifs were stitched around their edges using a discreet slip stitch or a decorative blanket or herringbone stitch. As the motif was stitched in place the allowance was folded underneath using the point of the needle. Inward-pointing shapes would need a clip with scissors to the point of the 'V' to facilitate the turning and outward curves may need clips taken out. However, as the motif fabric was well worn and soft, finger pressing was all that was usually needed. Where a stem or motif was narrow, a piece of the original fabric was left, which would blend with the new background.

A normal sewing needle was used with cotton sewing thread in a colour to tone with the motifs. Black or dark brown was used with the block prints as the stitches disappeared into the black outline. The work was held in the hand and when all the motifs were securely fixed in place the tacking stitches were removed.

Sometimes details like flower centres, veins on leaves and thorns on rose stems were added afterwards with coloured embroidery silks. These details would use simple stitches like chain, straight and French knots. The Broderie Perse bedcovers were very rarely quilted, padded or lined.

Ruins in a Chinese landscape
1820–1830
107½ x 113¾in (273 x 289cm)

THIS is the centre motif of a large bedcover that has a netted flounce on three sides. The scene is cleverly devised from various furnishing fabrics that had a chinoiserie theme and a Roman temple print. The floral motifs form a generous border on three sides.

The appliqué motifs are held to the linen ground with tiny slip stitches worked with black cotton thread. There are French knots worked in the centres of the flowers and chain stitches following the lines of the stems.

Drawing of the complete bedcover.

The centre motif showing ruins in a Chinese landscape.

Detail of the floral border.

Slip stitch

Fold the motif's allowance to the underneath with the tip of the needle and hold in place with the thumb. Knot the end of the thread and bring the needle up just through the motif's folded edge.

Take the needle down through the background fabric, very close to the motif, and up again through the folded edge about 2–3mm away. Repeat. The stitches should be small, neat and precisely follow the shape of the motif. The allowance is folded under as stitches are worked.

The stitches should be firm enough so that the motif cannot move but not so tight as to form puckers on the background.

Close up details showing small slip stitches and embroidery details.

Slip stitching and embroidery detailing of a Broderie Perse flower.

Slip stitches are neat and precise

French knots were used to embellish the centres of flowers

2–3mm seam allowance

Seam allowance clipped

Stem ends were tucked under the flower motifs

At narrow areas a bit of the original background fabric was left in place

Combined appliqué and pieced patchwork

As the supply of Indian prints became scarce, early 19th century dress fabrics become the fashionable choice for appliqué and patchwork. The bed- and cot cover on the following pages, made by the same hand, illustrate how delightfully simple appliqué shapes can be combined with pieced patchwork.

Nancy Horsfall's wedding bedcover

1833, 119½ x 118¾in (304 x 302cm)

The complete wedding bedcover.

*'Nancy Horsfall is my Name
England is my nation.
Tysehouse is my Dwelling place!
And Christ is my salvation.*

1833

*When I am dead and in my grave,
And all my bones are gone to dust
Take up this work and think of me!
When I am quite forgot.'*

INSCRIPTION ON NANCY HORSFALL'S
WEDDING COVERLET, 1833

NANCY Horsfall's wedding coverlet has the inscription above worked in cross stitch on a central panel of evenweave linen. This panel has appliquéd flower and leaf shapes and is edged with a pieced Vandyke border.

The cover grows bigger as each border is added. The first has leaf and buds with centred hearts. The second has six-pointed stars applied to pieced squares arranged on point. The third has alternate leaves and crosses with heart-shaped flowers at the corners. The fourth has large flower and leaf motifs with pieced eight-pointed stars at the corners. The final border is brown and pink chintz, which is flat quilted to hold it to the cotton ground. This is the only quilting on the whole coverlet as all the applied motifs and pieced shapes are slip stitched to the plain cotton background. Nancy's motifs are very simple and would be derived from freely drawn templates or even cutting directly into the fabric. None of the shapes is identical. The curved shapes would be easy to turn back and stitch to the background cloth. Each border strip was worked separately and then assembled at the end. This way the work in hand would be of a manageable size. All the seams are run and fell so there are no raw edges showing on either side. The hem edges of the chintz and the background are turned in and overstitched together.

Inscription in the centre of the bedcover.

Detail of hearts and leaves from the first layer of the border.

Nancy Horsfall is my Name
England is my nation.
Tysehouse is my Dwelling place !
And Christ is my Salvation.

1833

when i am dead and in my grave.
And all my bones are gone to dust
Take up this work and think of me !
when i am quite forgot.

Irregular hexagon motifs help make up the border.

The first part of the inscription, Welcome sweet babe.

Nancy Horsfall's baby's cot cover

1834

34 x 45in (86.5 x 114cm)

'Welcome sweet babe

Hush my dear be still and slumber
Holy angels gard thy head
Heavenly blessings without number
Gently falling on thy head 1834'

INSCRIPTION ON NANCY HORSFALL'S BABY'S COT COVER, 1834

JUST one year later, in 1834, Nancy Horsfall was stitching a cot cover for her new baby. In the same style as her wedding coverlet, this cover was not quilted. The pieced and appliqué shapes are neatly slip stitched to a plain cotton ground.

The Vandyke border is used again, this time to surround some flowers and leaves cut from some precious 18th century block-printed fabric. The other prints are small-scale, roller-printed dress fabrics, of which only a few have faded with time. The dedication and verse are worked on pieces of fine evenweave linen, ten cross stitches to each ³⁄₈in (1cm).

The border has squares presented on point with a motif made of four irregular hexagons applied to the centres. Eight-pointed stars decorate the corner blocks. The cot cover is bound with natural linen cloth.

welcome ✤ sweet ✤ babe

ᴍush my dear lie still and slumber
ᴍoly angels gard thy head
ᴍeavenly blessings without number
ɢentley falling on thy head 1834

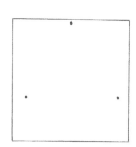

1

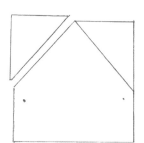

2

3

Vandyke borders

The Vandyke border was very popular in the 1830s and similar pointed trims appear on fashionable dress.

To construct the Vandyke border:

1 Cut the fabric into 3¼ x 3¼in (8 x 8cm) squares. Mark the centre top edge and side seams, 1¼in (3cm) from the bottom edge, with a pencil dot, allowing ¼in (0.5cm) seam allowance.

2 Trim off the top corners.

3 Put the right sides together, seam with a running stitch to the dot.

4 Open out the seam and finger press. Fold over the seam allowance and finger press to the wrong side.

5 Apply the edging to the ground fabric with neat slip stitches, putting one stitch exactly on the point. The bottom raw edge will be enclosed in the seam of the next border or hem.

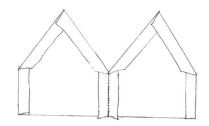

4

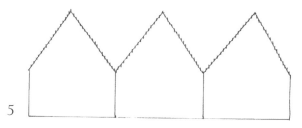

5

Eight-pointed stars

The template for the eight-pointed star may have been purchased or drafted from a square of folded paper at home. The star centre would be quite easy to seam and the seam allowance on the points was turned under and pressed before applying to the background. Draft the templates for an eight-pointed star by the folding paper method shown opposite.

1 Cut a square of paper a quarter of the size of the finished star.

2 Fold in half diagonally.

Detail of an eight-pointed star at the corner of the fourth layer of the border.

3 Fold point **B** to meet the side **A–C**.

4 Open the last fold out.

5 Fold point **C** to meet side **A–B**.

6 Fold point **B** back along line **C–F**.

7 Open up the last fold and fold point A back along side **C–E**.

8 Open up the square of paper. Carefully draw over the creased shapes with a ruler and shape 1 becomes the diamond template, square 2 is the corner template and triangle 3 is the side template.

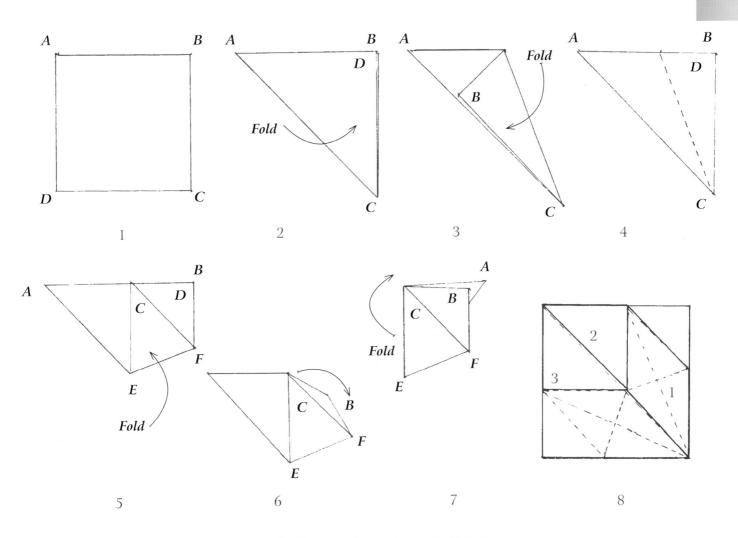

Note that seam allowances must be added to all of the pieces when cutting out the fabric shapes.

CASE STUDY

Early appliqué work

Appliqué table cover
1780–1820
43 x 46½in (109 x 118cm)

This table cover is about 200 years old but looks as though it was designed yesterday. It is unlined and the background consists of alternate stripes of fine cream cotton fabric and blue printed cloth. All the seams are sewn using the run and fell method, which encloses the raw edges completely.

The motifs are applied using the same technique as when stitching Broderie Perse. They are all cut from contemporary dress fabrics and the choice of colour and print is both subtle and distinctive. The central medallion is carefully constructed and the initials of the embroiderer are recorded in the middle, I.B.

The central medallion shows the initials of the embroiderer.

The hem edge has the same Vandyke border as Nancy Horsfall's cot cover, except the points are cut in pairs. The hem edge of the border and the background are turned in and slip stitched together to form the hem. The stitching, using cream cotton sewing thread, is so fine as to be almost invisible.

The complete table cover showing central medallion and alternate striped background.

The run and fell seams enclose raw edges completely.

Detail of the appliqué motifs.

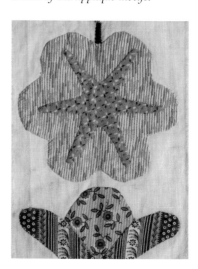

The appliqué bows

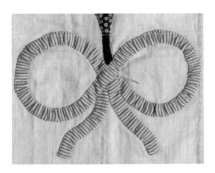

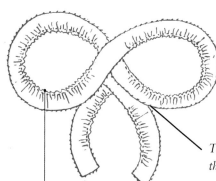

*The ends are hidden under
the loops of the bows.*

*The strips are cut on the grain of the
fabric and the long raw edges are turned
in 5mm.*

*The inner curves are gathered with tiny running stitches which
are pulled tight to curve the strip into shape before stitching
down with a slip stitch.*

Run and fell seams

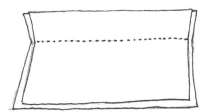

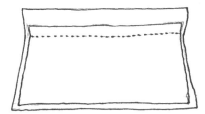

*1 The background strips are place right sides together
and sewn with a small running stitch.*

*2 The seam allowance on one side of the seam is
trimmed close to the stitching.*

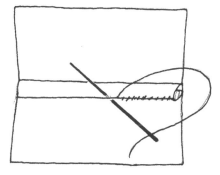

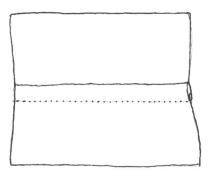

*3 The wide seam allowance is folded over twice to
enclose the narrow seam allowance. It is stitched down
with a small slip stitch. (Fell means hem in old
English.)*

*4 On the right side the seam is neat and tidy, on the
wrong side there are no raw edges showing.*

Template patchwork

'All the best patchwork is carried out with silk, satin, and velvet, either material entirely, or silk and velvet together, or satin and velvet together; not silk and satin mixed; and cotton fabric and silk should never be mingled in the same piece of work.'
WELDON'S PRACTICAL SHILLING GUIDE TO FANCY WORK, 1885

Silk, satin and velvet patchwork was the favourite of the Victorian needlewoman from the 1860s onwards. No home was complete without a bedspread, table cover, cushion or tea cosy worked in template patchwork.

Sumptuous offcuts from the local dressmaker were purchased and the new aniline-dyed silks were set against dark backgrounds so that the patches glowed like jewels.

The designs

THE designs had to be based on interlocking shapes and ladies' magazines offered many variations. Most were based on hexagons or diamonds derived from a hexagonal base or combinations of octagons and squares. Patterns that gave a three-dimensional effect were very popular.

Historical threads

Unfortunately many of these silk and satin patchwork examples have the odd patch that has disintegrated beyond repair. Silks and satins were bought by weight and the manufacturers would finish their cloth in a lead rinse, which made the fabric heavier. It is this metal residue that literally rotted away the fabric.

Honeycomb pattern with diamond rosettes

Simple diamond pattern

Box pattern

Right angle pattern

The patterns were given names such as 'honeycomb' and 'rosette' for the hexagonal designs, 'box' and 'attic window' for the three dimensional patterns. Complex designs comprising of many different shapes, such as long hexagons, squares and diamonds were called 'mosaics'.

Complex patterns that required different templates were found in ladies' magazines and shilling guides to fancy work. They were generally called 'mosaic' work.

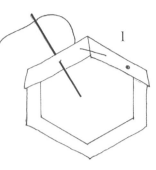

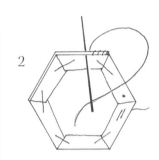

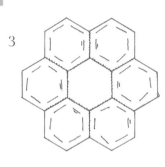

Method of working template patchwork

The patchwork design was chosen and the templates required accurately traced. These were transferred onto stiff card and carefully cut out. These cards were laid onto paper, traced around with a pencil and cut out. Many types of paper were used, such as old catalogues, which are often still in place in unfinished projects and are a great help in dating the work.

Next, the fabric pieces were cut out, approximately ¼in (0.5cm) bigger than the papers all round. The fabric was tacked to the papers, turning the seam allowance over the paper edge and to the wrong side. The tacking stitches were started with a knot and secured at the end with one back stitch. When sufficient pieces were tacked they could be arranged into the design layout on a flat surface.

Taking two adjacent pieces, with right sides together, the patches were seamed by over stitching with a strong sewing thread. The needle just caught the edges of the folded fabric and did not go through the papers.

The sewing was started with a knot, hidden under the seam allowance, and a couple of stitches on top of one another and ended the same way with three stitches. A normal sharps needle was used for all the sewing. As the work progressed, any patchwork pieces that were completely enclosed could have the tacking stitches cut and the papers removed. The paper shapes could then be used again.

1   The fabric is tacked on to the paper shape.
2   Putting right sides together, the pieces are overstitched.
3   When enclosed, the tacking stitches can be cut and the paper removed.

Unfinished hexagonal quilt

begun circa 1860 and added to in the 1880s

94½ x 108¼in (240 x 275cm)

THIS unfinished quilt still has the papers and tacking stitches intact. It is made of dress silks, some ikat weft-dyed, tartans, ginghams, ribbed woven, stripes, ombrés, figured brocades and fine velvets. The hexagons are stitched with tiny over stitches in black or neutral-coloured thread. It is a rosette design separated by single black hexagons. A hand-quilted, striped silk lining was prepared for the quilt which sadly was never completed.

The front of the unfinished hexagonal quilt.

Back of the unfinished quilt showing the papers and over stitching.

Unfinished quilt
1875–1900

THIS quilt is made of red flannel and cotton dress fabrics in the pattern known as 'boxes' or 'tumbling blocks'. The diamonds measure 3½in (9cm) from point to point. It is a valuable library of printed and woven dress fabrics dating back to the 1820s. Included are novelty prints, paisleys, woven shirting, ginghams and tiny engraved roller prints.

Details of the novelty prints used on the quilt, some dating back to the 1820s.

Four of the many ways that log cabin blocks can be arranged.

'Barn Raising' or 'Square on Point'

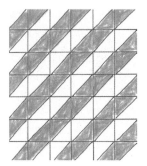

'Straight Furrow' or 'Diagonal Lines'

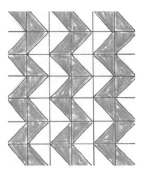

'Streaks of Lightning' or 'Zigzag'

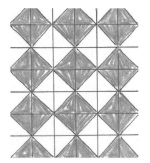

'Sunshine and Shadow' or 'Diamond Pattern'

Log cabin patchwork

Log cabin patchwork was introduced from North America and Canada. It was made from strips of fabric, often too narrow for any other purpose, and sometimes included ribbons. They were made of cotton prints, silks and velvets or woollen woven cloth. The 19th century method of construction was quite bulky and thus did not require any additional wadding or quilting to make a substantial quilt cover. However, there was usually a lining, which covered the construction seam of the blocks. When log cabin patchwork was used for a table cover, it was finished with a gathered flounce.

Log cabin designs

The dramatic impact of the log cabin patchwork entirely relied on the clever use of dark and light fabrics. Each block was divided diagonally into dark- and light-toned colours. The small square in the centre was a dark colour or a very bright colour depending on whether it was to recede or jump out of the overall design.

When the blocks were completed, they could be arranged in numerous ways; all gave totally different effects. Depending on how the blocks were set, diagonal, diamond or zigzag stripes emerged, as if by magic.

Alternative ways of constructing log cabin blocks

'Court House Steps' – the strips are stitched in pairs, opposite one another.

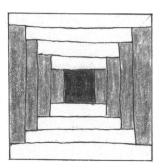

'Pineapple' – The strips alternate with rounds straight and rounds on the diagonal.

Typical measurements for a four-log block

Calico base – 8¼ x 8¼in (21 x 21cm), ¼in (1cm) seam allowance allowed for joining blocks

Centre square – 1½ x 1½in (4 x 4cm)

Strips – 1¼in (3cm) wide, ⅛in (0.5cm) seam allowance

The result is a four-log block, finished size 8 x 8in (20 x 20cm)

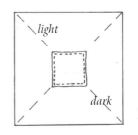

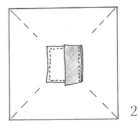

Method of working the basic log cabin block

The 19th century log cabin blocks were worked on a foundation of calico or cotton cloth. These squares were cut first, being the size of the finished block plus a seam allowance all round for sewing the blocks together.

The patchwork fabrics were sorted into two piles, dark and light tones. A colour scheme would have been selected but it was the tonal value that took priority. The fabrics were cut into equal-width strips. Ribbons, of the correct width, could also be used. A fabric was selected for the centres of the blocks and one small square was cut for each block.

Constructing a log cabin block

1   The calico squares were folded and creased diagonally as a guide to placing the centre square, which was stitched in place. A small running stitch was used throughout the construction of log cabin patchwork. The seams were started with a knot and a couple of overstitches and finished with three stitches on top of one another. Then one diagonal half was labelled as dark and the other as light.

2   A dark strip was laid on one edge of the centre square, right sides together. The seam was sewn and the strip folded back. If the fabric was thick, it was held down with tacking stitches. All the sewing was done using regular sewing thread and a sharps needle.

3   Moving clockwise around the block, another dark strip was sewn in the same manner, this time covering the centre square and the first strip.

4   This time a light strip was sewn in place, covering the centre block and the previous two strips. Most patchworkers did not cut the strips to length until they were sewn in place and could be trimmed accurately. This was a more economical way of working and led to a better, random colour selection.

5   The procedure was repeated with the fourth strip, which was a light one.

6   The alternating two light and two dark strips were sewn around the block until it was full.

7   There would be the same number of logs on the four sides but the number varied according to the availability of cloth, the width of the strips and the patience of the patchworker.

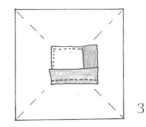

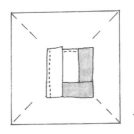

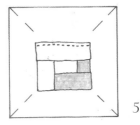

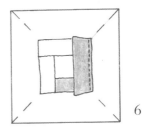

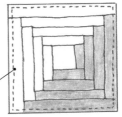

Seam allowance for joining blocks

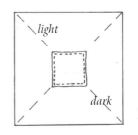

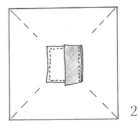

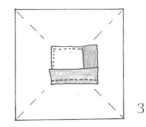

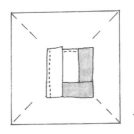

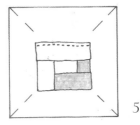

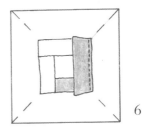

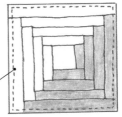

light

dark

1

2

3

4

5

6

7

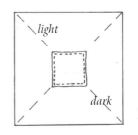

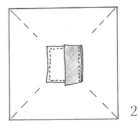

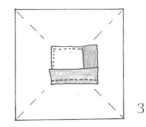

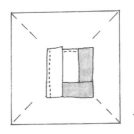

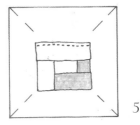

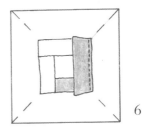

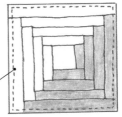

Log cabin carriage rug

circa 1880

59 x 43½in (150 x 111cm)

Detail of one block of the carriage rug showing the clever use of dark and light fabrics.

The 'straight furrows' create a diagonal effect.

THIS travel rug is worked in wool tweeds, wool challis, brushed cottons and shirting. Each block is 5in (12.5cm) square and the blocks are arranged in a diagonal set known as 'straight furrows'. The blocks are worked on a foundation of medium-weight calico.

The colour scheme looks very modern with its tans and greys contrasting with bright purples and touches of red. A very dramatic use is made of a black and white striped woollen cloth. The centre squares are black.

The rug is lined with a checked black and tan brushed cotton. The hem edges are tuned in with the lining and slipped stitched together. The rug is very heavy and certainly would have kept the draughts at bay.

Log cabin table cover

1860–1890

45½ x 46in (116 x 117cm)

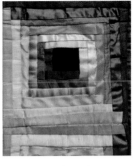

THIS table cover is made of silks, satins and velvet and breaks all the log cabin rules concerning light and dark tones. The centre squares are black velvet. The individual blocks shade from dark to light towards the centre and from light to dark into the corners. The blocks are grouped into fours and the whole effect makes the log cabin patchwork glow like a jewel.

'Many large linen drapers and silk merchants will sell bundles of remnants by the pound and pieces are often procurable from dressmakers.'

WELDON'S PRACTICAL SHILLING GUIDE TO FANCY WORK, 1885

Details of the large blocks showing the dramatic colour choice and the odd decorative silk ribbon amongst the fabric strips.

Each large block is 11½in (29cm) square. The cover is lined with rust-coloured silk and has a flounce of maroon and cream flocked cotton edging.

Crazy patchwork

'This consists of pieces of various coloured silk arranged in all shapes and sizes, the edges being turned in and the joins hidden by a row of fancy stitching worked in bright silk. It is also called Kaleidoscope or Japanese patchwork...'
WELDON'S PRACTICAL GUIDE TO FANCY WORK, 1885

Crazy patchwork was constructed from random scraps of silk, satin and velvet sewn onto a foundation of calico or cotton cloth. The patches were further embellished with little embroidered motifs. Some ladies' magazines offered small-scale transfers that were specifically for the use on crazy patchwork and some motifs appear regularly on various pieces from England and North America. The seams were covered with lines of embroidery, some based on feather or herringbone stitch and others more complex.

Unfinished crazy patchwork
1870–1890
29 x 41¾in (74 x 106cm)

The crazy patchwork made from dressmaking scraps. The detail shows the neat feather stitch seams.

THIS crazy patchwork is made of dressmaking scraps of a mix of woven, printed and plain silk fabrics. The piece is made of six blocks and most of the patches are under 3¼in (8cm) long and even as small as 1¼in (3cm). The patchwork is immaculately finished. A neat feather stitch is worked over all the seams with yellow cotton perlé embroidery thread.

Design

There were not any design limitations for crazy patchwork. Any scrap of fabric, whatever shape or size, could be used. The colour scheme was as random as possible and could depend on which piece came out of the 'bit bag' next. As the majority of crazy patchwork pieces are in silks and velvets there was no problems about washing or colours running, as the items would not be subject to laundering. The embroidery along the seams could be in one colour, yellow being the favourite, or a different coloured thread on each seam. The motifs were similarly treated. The threads used for the embroidery were stranded cottons, cotton perlés or 'Filoselle'; a silk stranded thread, which was particularly recommended for a rich and shiny effect.

Tea cosy

circa 1880

Width 15¼in (39cm), height 10½in (27cm)

THIS large and heavy tea cosy is made of small patches of dress silks, many of which are embroidered with little motifs. There is a wide selection of silk velvets, damasks, checks, stripes and even ribbons amongst the choice of patchwork pieces. A neat feather stitch in gold-coloured perlé thread covers the seams. The tea cosy is lined with a plum-coloured, quilted cotton sateen and edged with a plum and gold cord.

Crazy patchwork tea cosy made from dress silks. The detail (below) shows an embroidered motif.

Historical threads

This form of bizarre patchwork was very fashionable from around 1870 till the end of the century. Crazy patchwork is found not only on bed quilts but was used for table covers, cushions, tea cosies, work bags and all manner of fancy articles for the home.

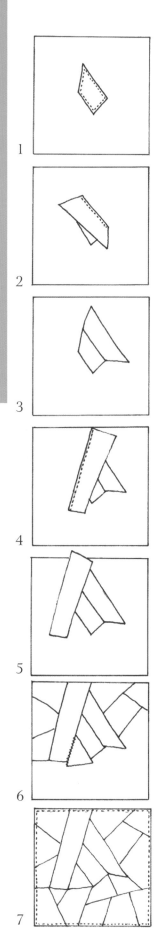

Method of working crazy patchwork

A base of calico or plain cotton was required and this was cut into squares the size of the finished block plus a seam allowance for assemblage. With small projects, such as tea cosies, the calico was cut to the shape of the pattern. Keeping the work small and manageable was the aim.

The fabric, if not already in small pieces, was cut into random shapes with straight sides. Triangles, strips and rhomboids were easier to fit together. Any embroidered motifs were worked at this stage or possibly on a larger piece of fabric. This could be stretched in a small hoop to work the embroidery and then cut down to size. The embroidered motifs used the usual basic stitches but ribbon work flowers gave another effect.

1 The first patch was laid in the centre of the calico square and tacked or pinned into place.

2 The second patch was placed, right sides together, along the straight edge of the first patch. The seam was sewn with a small running stitch through all the layers. Regular sewing thread and a sharps needle was used. The stitching started with a knot and ended with a couple of overstitches. There would be no stress on the seams, as the embroidered lines would strengthen them.

3 The second patch was folded back and held in place with a pin.

4 The third patch was added along a straight edge and folded back.

5 If the patches overlapped the base square, they were trimmed off. Patches could be trimmed into more suitable shapes as work progressed.

6 Work continued adding random shapes. If a 'V' or an 'L' shape was left uncovered a small piece could be slip stitched over the existing pieces to fill the gap.

7 When the whole square was filled, the edges were secured with a running stitch.

Seam stitches for crazy patchwork

The stitches worked over or next to the seams were usually the simple stitches like feather, chevron and herringbone as they were quick to work and easier to keep an even tension when stitching through a few layers of cloth. Complex stitches were also used but these were mainly variations of chain, lazy daisy, straight and herringbone stitches with exotic names.

A sample of stitches used over the seams of crazy patchwork

Fly stitch with additional straight stitches.

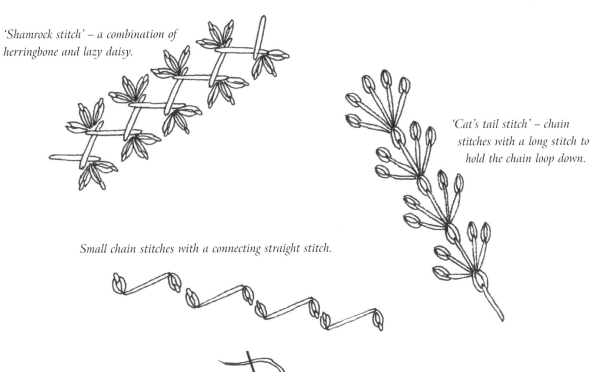

'Shamrock stitch' – a combination of herringbone and lazy daisy.

'Cat's tail stitch' – chain stitches with a long stitch to hold the chain loop down.

Small chain stitches with a connecting straight stitch.

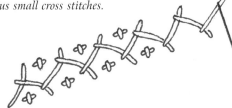

Herringbone with the needle held at right angles to the line of stitching plus small cross stitches.

Lazy daisy chain stitch worked in pairs.

Lazy daisy with straight stitch leaves.

Herringbone with additional straight stitches.

Lazy daisy grouped into flower and leaf shapes.

Chevron stitch stage 1.

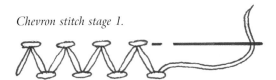

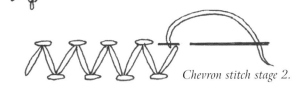

Chevron stitch stage 2.

Fancy Work

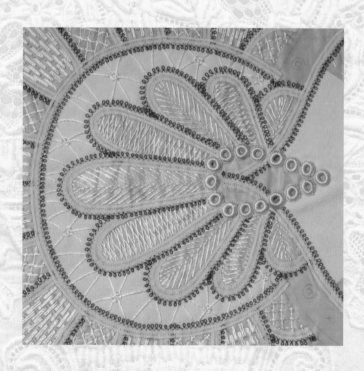

'Another argument for busying good women in the works of
fancy is, because it takes them off from scandal, the usual
attendant of tea-tables and all other inactive scenes of life...
A third reason I shall mention is, the profit that is brought
to the family when these pretty arts are encouraged.
It is manifest that this way of life not only keeps fair ladies
from running out into expenses but is at the same time
an actual improvement.'
THE ART OF NEEDLEWORK, The Countess of Wilton, 1840

ELDON'S *Practical Shilling Guide to Fancy Work*, 1885, contains instructions for knitted stockings and crochet evening bags, patchwork and crewel work, smocking and canvas work, macramé and bead work. Other chapters gave instructions on the decorative use of ribbons and braids for household items and personal dress. These techniques formed an important part of the Victorian needlewoman's repertoire.

As weaving technology advanced in the 19th century, many attractive braids and ribbons were manufactured copying the exquisite handmade versions of the past. As these new trims became more readily available, embroidery techniques involving simple methods and stitches were developed. Thus the amateur needlewoman could stitch dress embellishments and dainty trimmings that previously required a professional embroiderer.

Black wool tea cosy

circa 1875

Height 11in (28cm), width 16½in (42cm)

THIS very smart tea cosy is decorated with a soutache braid, which has been dyed in a variegated fashion from cream to bright pink. It has a diamond quilted, black cotton sateen lining and all the seams are edged with a heavy crimson furnishing cord, which finishes with a tassel on top.

Black wool tea cosy with soutache braid.

Soutache work

Soutache work, also known as 'braid work', was an attractive way of decorating clothes and household accessories. It did not require exceptional needle skills or hours of dedicated embroidery work.

The narrow braid, often called 'Russian braid', was constructed by plaiting threads around a two-stranded, cotton-core base. It was usually only about $^1/_8$in (2–3mm) wide and extremely flexible, which meant it could be manipulated around tight curves and remain flat. It was manufactured in many colours and in a shiny silk or a matt cotton finish. The cotton variety was more suitable for items that needed to be laundered.

The construction of the soutache or Russian braid.

Baby's carrying cape
1880–1885
Full length 36in (91.5cm)

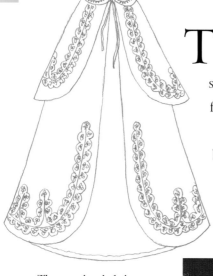

The complete baby's carrying cape, 1880–1885.

This cape is made of fine blue merino wool and the hem borders have an elaborate soutache design that is entirely hand-sewn with little back stitches. The design, reminiscent of Celtic knot work, was produced from one continuous line.

The baby's cloak was a very popular garment for braid work and could be displayed when baby was held in the arms for an outing in the park.

Very young babies were dressed in cream wool capes with matching soutache work. Older babies were wrapped in bright blues and red capes, often with contrasting braid work.

Detail of the carrying cape showing the elaborate soutache design.

Designs for soutache work

The patterns for soutache work had to be curvaceous and based on a continuous line. To be obliged to keep cutting the braid would have been tedious and time consuming. The patterns were available as transfers and could be purchased at the repositories or were enclosed in monthly magazines. The preferred background for silk soutache work was a slightly felted, merino wool cloth. This matt fabric showed off the shiny braid work beautifully. Cotton soutache braid was sewn on to cotton cloth and was used for children's summer clothes and bedroom accessories such as cases, toilette bags and capes used to protect the shoulders when brushing hair.

Detail of the soutache work showing the small backstitches used to fix the braid in position.

Boy's red wool dress
1855–1860

THIS red wool dress is hand-stitched with black silk soutache braid. The pattern is composed of one continuous line. The garment is styled with a mock jacket and would be worn over a shirt. It fastens up the centre back with hooks and eyes with decorative silk bows at the neck and waist.

Historical threads

Young boys were kept in 'skirts' for as long as possible and these were worn over pantaloons which often had a frill or pleated trim. Only at the age of four to five years would boys be allowed to wear knee-length trousers.

Method of stitching soutache work

The design was drawn onto the fabric or an iron-on transfer could be used. Alternatively the pattern was drawn on thin paper. This was tacked to the background fabric, the braid attached and then the paper torn away.

The route of the braid had to be decided first. If the design dictated that the braid went under a line already stitched, a gap would have to be left so that the braid could be threaded underneath. However, this refinement was not often used, as it would interrupt the flow of applying the braid.

An ordinary sewing needle was used with matching silk thread. A back stitch with a small space between stitches was preferred as this was more durable than a simple running stitch. The stitches would sink into the middle of the braid, between the inner string cores, and be almost invisible.

'The pattern should be drawn on silver paper, which is tacked on the piece of work, and the braid worked on it with the same coloured sewing silk, as thread washes white. To sew on silk braid, you should use silk drawn out of the braid, as it is finer and more even, and will match the colour better than any other you can procure; cut off, therefore, a bit the length of a needleful, to keep for the purpose of unroving.'

THE WORKWOMAN'S GUIDE, by a Lady, 1830

By the early 1860s many dressmakers owned sewing machines and much of the soutache work in the 1870s and 1880s was applied by machine. An attachment, in the form of a loop, was fixed to the machine foot and this guided the braid into place. The intricate looped patterns were still produced but the precision of the handwork was lost in the process.

Back stitching the soutache braid onto the material.

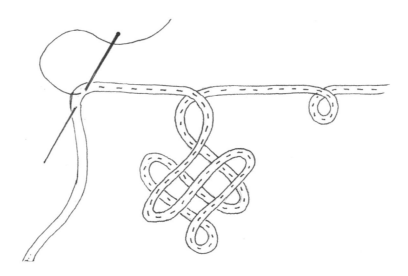

Shoulder cape with a collar

circa 1885

Length at centre front 14½in (37cm)

T HE back and front views of this gold-coloured cape, made of felted wool cloth, show an intricate soutache pattern applied with a lock stitch machine. The front edges have borders of decorative brass buttons and the cape fastens with four large hooks and eyes. The cape has a matching satin lining.

The shoulder cape as it would have been worn.

Details of the intricate soutache work on the front and back of the cape.

Soutache work cape in felted wool.

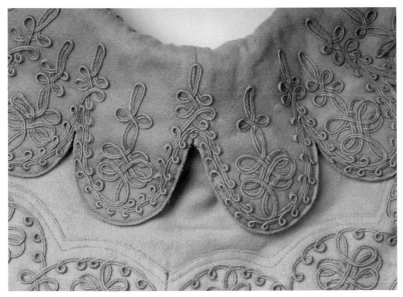

A condensed history of the sewing machine

A machine that could sew continuous seams obsessed many inventors during the 19th century as a constant supply of army uniforms were required, as well as fashionable clothes. This timeline shows the progression that they made.

- **1830** – Bartholemy Thimmonier patented a chain stitch machine. It had an arm, a vertical hooked needle and a presser foot which held the fabric in a horizontal position. His 80 machines, installed in Paris, were smashed to pieces by French tailors and dressmakers who feared the end of their livelihood.

- **1834** – Walter Hunt invented a lock stitch machine. Like machines today, it used a spool thread above and a shuttle below. His needle was curved with an eye at the pointed end but the feed was not continuous and the fabric had to be reset on a metal track for all but the shortest seams.

- **1846** – Elias Howe invented a lock stitch machine and the fabric travelled vertically, held by pins on a metal plate. By 1862, he had a huge factory and made a fortune supplying the clothing industry with sewing machines.

- **1850** – Isaac Singer perfected Howe's ideas with a vertical straight needle that moved up and down, a presser foot, shuttle mechanism and a wheel that moved the fabric. The modern sewing machine was born. Singer also developed the treadle mechanism that freed both hands.

- **1854** – Allen B Wilson designed the rotary hook shuttle and the four-motion feed, known as the 'feed dog', that pushed the fabric along whilst sewing. Both these mechanisms are standard on modern machines today.

- **1858** – Singer had designed 'Family' models for use in the home. He also introduced 'hire purchase' so that they could be paid for in instalments.

As well as in America, domestic machines were being developed in Europe and Great Britain. 1862 – Pfaff of Germany, 1864 – Frister & Rossman of Berlin, 1864 – Jones of England, 1872 – Viking-Husqvarna of Sweden and 1893 – Bernina of Switzerland.

The 'Little Wanzer' sewing machine, 1870–1890.
It was used in all National Schools in Ireland for
training young girls in machine and dressmaking skills.

Renaissance lace

'Renaissance Braid Work – This is also known as Renaissance Lace, and is really only a Modern Point Lace, worked with a very Open Braid, and with only one stitch as a Filling, instead of several.'

THE DICTIONARY OF NEEDLEWORK, SFA Caulfield & BC Saward, 1885

This type of braid work was known by various names. Mrs Beeton called this technique 'point lace' and Thérèse de Dillmont referred to it as 'Irish lace'. Generally it is referred to as 'Renaissance lace' as it essentially imitates the 16th and 17th century laces that were made from a handmade bobbin lace braid that was sewn together as it was constructed. The 19th century version used narrow machine-made braids that varied from straight and plain to those with curves and scallops or dainty picot edges.

Renaissance lace was not hardwearing and therefore was not suitable for children's clothes or complete garments. It was mainly used for cuffs, collars and other dress accessories such as fans. Fashionable from the 1830s till the end of the century, it was the enterprising needlewoman's replacement for expensive bobbin and needlepoint lace.

Designs for Renaissance lace

Similar to the soutache work, the patterns for the Renaissance lace were constructed of curving and if possible continuous lines. The spaces between the lines were designed so that the connecting bars were not too long, as this would produce a slipshod piece of lace.

The patterns were purchased ready traced on glazed cotton fabric. If pre-prepared designs were not available they could be traced with Indian ink on to a stiff fabric or architect's tracing cloth. Some patterns only showed the track of the braids and it was left to the embroiderer to work out the connecting bars and fillings that had to be worked to hold the lace together. Other patterns, usually the simpler designs, show clearly where the bars are to be placed and give a suggestion of the detached buttonhole stitches and fillings on a small section of the drawing.

Braids were available in many widths from 5/64in (2mm) up to 25/64in (10mm). The best quality braids were woven from linen thread. They came in many variations and those with a regular narrow and wide repeat could

Historical threads

Thérèse de Dillmont was born in Austria in 1846. Thérèse may have received training at the Royal School of Art Needlework as later, with her sister, she opened an embroidery studio and workshop. As her needlework career progressed she moved to Mulhouse in Alsace, the home of DMC (Dollfus-Mieg et Cie), producers of quality embroidery and lacemaking threads since 1841. Thérèse went on to produce a series of books on needlework techniques for DMC but she is most well known for her *Encyclopedia of Needlework*, used for generations of embroiderers up to the present day. Thérèse died in 1890.

be manipulated into flower and leaf shapes. They were manufactured in black, white and a neutral cream colour. If another colour was required then the finished item would have to be dyed.

Two Renaissance lace border designs that clearly show both the guidelines for the braid and the connecting bars.

Historical threads

Isabella Beeton, born in 1836, published her famous *Mrs Beeton's Book of Household Management* in 1861. *Mrs Beeton's Book of Needlework* was published in 1870, five years after her death. It covers many interesting techniques, including 'point lace'. The knitting and crochet chapters are taken from books written by Mrs Mee in the 1860s. The tatting chapter is likewise copied from an earlier publication by Miss Austin.

Method of working Renaissance lace

The braids were tacked along the guidelines of the pattern. However, the lace braid was not flexible and had to be neatly folded at any corners and eased around curves. The easing was accomplished by working little gathering stitches on the inner curves. Little whipping stitches were worked along the edge of the braid and the fullness was gently pulled into shape. This shaping was done after the braid was tacked into place.

The only stitches that were actually worked through the pattern were the tacking stitches. All other stitches were worked 'in the air' catching the edges of the braids with the needle but skimming over the pattern.

Once the braids were in place, the connecting bars were made with a single straight stitch or one that was overcast. Thicker bars could be made with two or three stitches that were then covered with buttonhole stitch and sometimes incorporated picots. The detached buttonhole fillings are similar to those used on Ayrshire embroidery but on a much larger scale.

The threads used were linen, cotton twist or even silk in a colour to match the braids. The work was held in the hand and the stiffness of the pattern kept the stitches at an even tension.

When all the needlepoint fillings and bars were completed the work was turned over and the tacking stitches were cut. The lace was carefully pulled away from the pattern and any bits of tacking thread that remained were then removed.

Unfinished Renaissance lace
late 19th century

THE pattern, number 17167, is printed on to a strip of blue glazed cotton fabric. The braid is being tacked into place and some of the filling stitches and connecting bars have been worked. Only in the section about to be worked are the suggested filling stitches and bars drawn on the pattern.

Renaissance lace work in progress.

Applying the braid

The braid is tacked on to the pattern

Neat folds were made at the corners

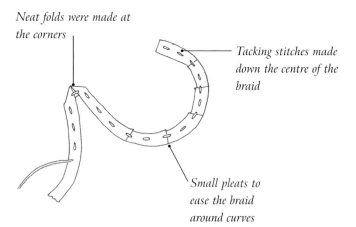

Tacking stitches made down the centre of the braid

Small pleats to ease the braid around curves

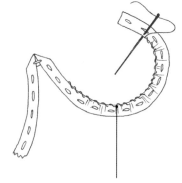

The inside edge of the braid is gathered to remove the pleats and ease the fullness

Needlepoint fillings

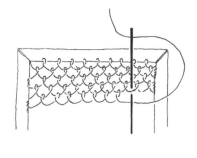

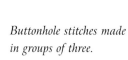

Simple buttonhole stitch, the thread is whipped down the side of the braid to reach the position for the next row.

Buttonhole stitches made in groups of three.

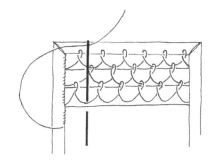

Buttonhole stitch with the return row as a straight stitch, which is incorporated into the next row.

'The needles employed are usually Messrs. Walker's needles, Nos. 9 and 10. The scissors should be small, sharp and pointed. An ivory thimble may be safely employed in this light work.'

MRS BEETON'S BOOK OF NEEDLEWORK, 1870

Bars used in Renaissance lace

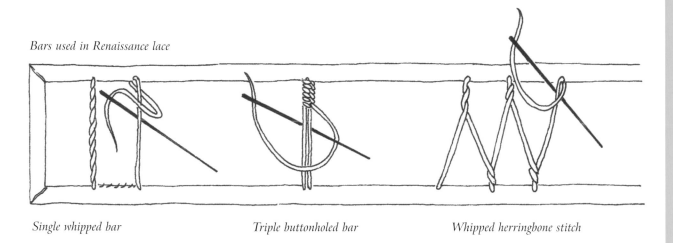

Single whipped bar   Triple buttonholed bar   Whipped herringbone stitch

Sampler

1870–1890

6 x 4in (15 x 10cm)

THIS small sampler shows a variety of needlepoint fillings and bars intended for Renaissance lace. The grid is made from strips of braid. The sampler is tacked onto pink glazed cotton further stiffened by a layer of brown paper.

Sampler, 1870–1890, showing a variety of needlepoint fillings and bars.

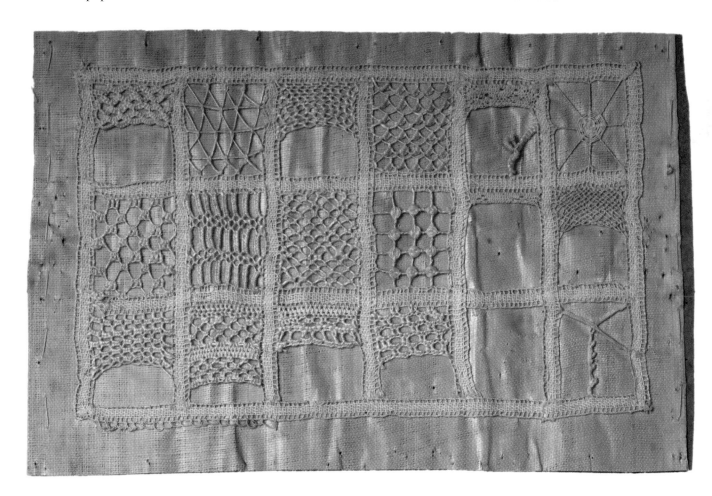

Renaissance lace fan

1880–1890

Sticks 10½in (27cm) long

THIS delicate lace fan is made from a very narrow braid, only ¼in (5mm) wide, which twists and turns to create delightful flower shapes. The buttonhole bars are worked with a central picot. There are a variety of dainty needlepoint fillings. The sticks are mother of pearl.

*Renaissance lace fan,
1880–1890.*

*Detail of the Renaissance
lace fan showing the
intricate twists and turns
of the flower shapes.*

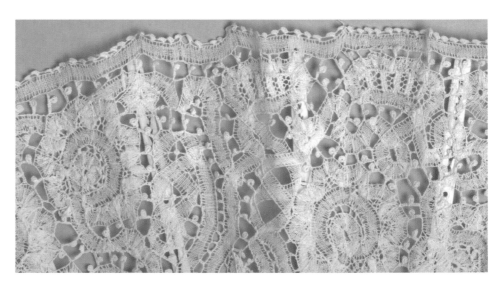

Table runner

circa 1890

13¾ x 51in (35 x 130cm)

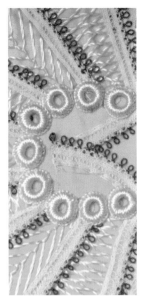

Detail of the table runner.

Unfinished flannel and yellow silk table runner, circa 1890.

THIS unfinished table runner shows another, rather unusual, technique using the Renaissance lace braids. The background is a layer of cream wool flannel. Over this was placed a layer of fine yellow silk that was printed with the design. The linen braid was applied along the pattern lines with a small back stitch. The braid is made of linen thread but has a black picot edging along one side.

The leaf shapes have been filled with a wide herringbone and feather stitch worked in shiny filoselle silk thread. By wrapping the thread around a large knitting needle a few times a ring was formed and buttonhole stitched all round. This is the same method as used by the Ayrshire workers to make their 'pearls', but on a much larger scale. Finally, the yellow silk was carefully cut away leaving quite a dramatic effect.

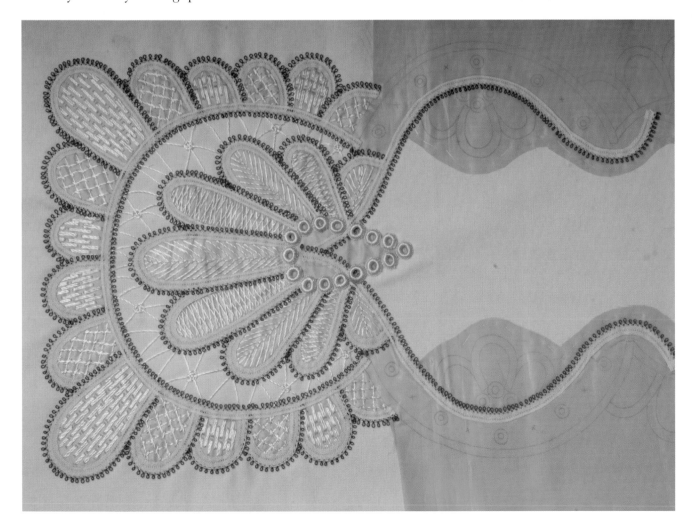

Ribbon embroidery

Ribbon embroidery was very popular in the late 18th century, when it was used to decorate small bags, needle cases, pincushions and the fronts of gentlemen's waistcoats. It had a tremendous revival in the late 19th century when the earlier techniques were rediscovered and the specialist ribbons required were being manufactured in every colour imaginable.

Although referred to as 'China' ribbons, where they originated from in the 18th century, the narrow ribbons were produced in England and France in the 19th century. The ribbons were also used for bookmarks in the book-binding trade.

This form of embroidery was quick to work and produced a very effective piece of work without having to practise and perfect one's sewing skills. As ribbon embroidery was unsuitable for washing it appears on decorative household items, often protected by glass, or evening dress and accessories.

Oval fire screen

Oval panel for a pole-style fire screen.

1880–1890, 11¼ x 13¾in (28.5 x 35cm)

THIS oval panel was intended for a pole-style fire screen and has an elegant design reminiscent of the Rococo period. Most of the coloured ribbons are shaded. The simple straight stitch is used creatively to form petals and leaves with French knot centres. The central bunch of flowers is finished with a couched gold thread. The background is pale blue moiré silk.

Detail showing the coloured ribbon work.

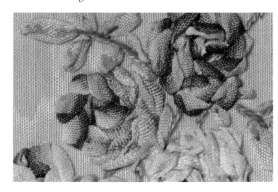

Ribbon embroidery designs and materials

The designs were available in magazines and from the needlework shops. Many were produced as iron-on transfers. They usually offered instruction as to the stitches to use and which parts should be worked in ribbons and which in embroidery silks.

The ribbons were available in many shades and colours, including shaded ones that changed from dark to light across the width or variegated ones that changed colour along the length. The most popular ribbons were:

'**Pompadour**' – ⅛in (3mm) wide and in self-shades, shaded and variegated.

'**Giant Crêpe**' – ½in (13mm) wide and had a slightly crinkled surface.

'**Picotee**' – ⅝in (17mm) wide, was serrated on one edge and was used for gathered flowers.

To begin a piece, the embroiderer would have to have a good selection of ribbons and coordinating embroidery silks. An assortment of beads, sequins and possibly gold thread might also be required.

The fabric was stretched in a hoop or a frame for all the stitching. This was necessary, as the other hand was needed to manipulate the ribbon and stop it from twisting. The floral motifs should appear to float on the surface of the fabric so that they look almost three dimensional and daintily realistic. Ribbon embroidery was usually worked on a silk fabric but fine net was fashionable for evening gowns.

'The best patterns are those that introduce flowers of the forget-me-not size, small roses and bluebells, as, although the work does in no way attempt to be natural, it should never offend by being executed in large designs; when worked in small patterns, it has a quaint, old-fashioned look which it cannot retain when enlarged.'
THE DICTIONARY OF NEEDLEWORK, SFA Caulfield & BC Saward, 1885

For the ribbon embroidery, a chenille needle was required with a sharp point to pierce the fabric and an eye large enough to accommodate the ribbon. Sharps needle were needed for any couched ribbon work. Crewel needles were used for the silk embroidery and fine bead needles for sequins and tiny beads.

Two designs for ribbon embroidery motifs showing clearly how to stitch the ribbons to form the petals.

Drawstring bag

circa 1850

8½ x 9in (22 x 23cm)

An early example of dainty ribbon embroidery worked on black satin. Most of the flowers have been worked with a couple of straight stitches but manage to capture the essence of the flower shapes. The roses are worked using the looped method. The bag is edged with black 'blonde lace' and is lined with black silk.

Drawstring bag with ribbon embroidery on black satin.

Detail of the ribbon work flowers.

Ribbon embroidery stitches and techniques

All the stitches were worked using a stabbing up and down motion through the fabric. When stitching the ribbon through the fabric, it was important that the ribbon did not twist. Most of the skill in ribbon embroidery depended on the careful manipulation of the ribbon but luckily the stitches were very simple to work. A short length of ribbon was used in the needle and work was started with a knot on the wrong side of the fabric and finished in the same way. Any short bits of ribbon that were left over were saved for tiny accents like the centres of flowers.

On completion, the plain fabric areas could be ironed from the wrong side. However, pressing the ribbon embroidery would flatten the stitches and ruin the whole effect.

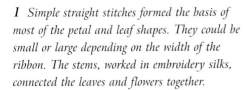

1 Simple straight stitches formed the basis of most of the petal and leaf shapes. They could be small or large depending on the width of the ribbon. The stems, worked in embroidery silks, connected the leaves and flowers together.

2 Wider petals were created by taking two stitches side by side or by catching the point with embroidery thread.

3 Small loops, the largest in the centre and the smallest at the edge, were grouped together to give a dome-shaped flower.

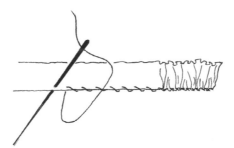

4 Straight stitches that were worked in rounds from the centre create a rosebud effect.

5 The wider ribbon was gathered by working little whipping stitches along one edge.

6 The gathered ribbon was back stitched in a spiral until the flower shape was filled.

Lazy daisy

French knots

Straight stitches of ribbon decorated with silk straight stitches

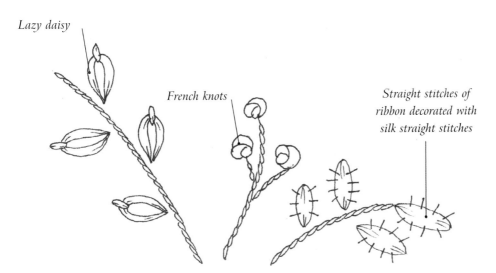

Other simple stitches were worked with the narrow ribbons, such as lazy daisy and French knots.

153

Evening gown and fan
1890

'Many of the latest and most exclusive of Parisian model gowns are lavishly trimmed with the daintiest of dainty ribbon embroidery, in the most alluring of colouring and designs.'

NEEDLECRAFT MAGAZINE, 1900

This magnificent ensemble consists of a bodice and skirt, a fan and a small bag. Stitched carefully by a mother for her daughter's venture into society, it is a outstanding example of ribbon embroidery. The dress is made of cream satin fabric and the front panels of the bodice and skirt are entirely covered in ribbon embroidery. The design is enhanced with the application of a couched double line of gold thread, which encloses little convex sequins. Two large bows on the skirt are held with paste buckles that are echoed in the paste buttons attached to the little semi-circular flaps on the bodice. 'Paste' is an 18th and 19th century term for glass jewels or imitation gems.

A large chiffon knot finishes the neckline and the ribbon work extends over the shoulders on the collar pieces. A cream silk fringe completes the hem of the skirt. The bodice is tightly fitted and laces up the centre back. The skirt is pleated at the back and falls into a sweeping train. Some of the major seams are decorated with a crinkled ribbon trim.

As well as this amazing undertaking, the ingenious mother made a matching 'Dorothy' drawstring bag and fan to go with her daughter's outfit. The fan has mother of pearl sticks and is embroidered in the same design as the front panels. The dress is machine sewn and was probably assembled by a professional dressmaker. Likewise, the fan was most likely sent to a fan maker to be constructed.

The matching ribbon work fan.

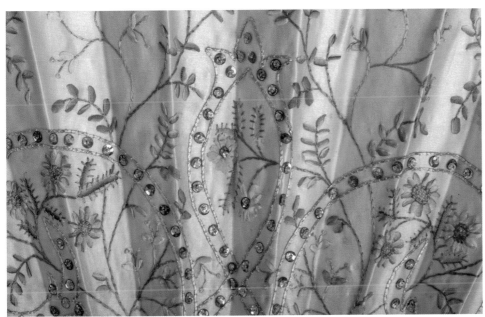

Detail of the fan showing the ribbon and sequin work.

The elaborate ribbon work evening gown.

155

CASE STUDY

The Misses Tottie's evening dresses

The Misses Tottie were twin sisters and these are their evening dresses, obviously intended for an important event. At the height of fashion and both made of silk net, they have a high waistline, low-cut small bodices, puffed sleeves and ankle-length skirts.

Blue evening dress
1822

The blue dress is trimmed with pale blue satin cut on the bias to make piped, curving ribbons that are supported by bunches of silk flowers. The bands on the bodice and sleeves are edged with blonde silk lace. The rolled satin hem is padded to hold the skirt in a gentle A-line and above this there is a swag of net held by pleated loops of the same blue satin. Although missing a lining or petticoat, the dress has survived well.

Detail of the hem and satin trim.

Pink evening dress
1822

In exactly the same style with the same padded hem, the pink dress is embroidered with a heavy border of couched chenille flowers. These are decorated with silver blown glass beads that are quite light individually but heavy when grouped in masses. The pink circles around the beads are made of silk thread wrapped around card shapes. Heavy pink silk cords are applied between the beads. All this weight has taxed the silk net fabric and the garment has disintegrated badly.

Details of the chenille and glass-beaded border.

Learning to Sew

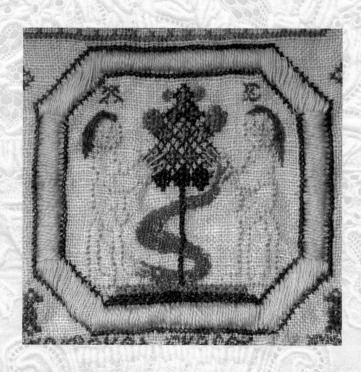

*'Besides I began personally to like some of the best girls;
and they like me. I had amongst my scholars several
farmers' daughters – young women grown, almost.
These could already read, write, and sew; and to them
I taught the elements of grammar, geography, history,
and the finer kinds of needlework.'*
JANE EYRE, Charlotte Brontë, 1847

EVERY 19th century young girl was taught to sew, whether by her mother, aunt, governess, school or orphanage. It was expected that upper-class girls would use their skills as an improving and gentile way of passing the time and produce a sampler worth framing to hang on the wall. Middle-class girls would be able to stitch a pictorial sampler, mend their clothes and mark household linen for laundry purposes. The working-class girls could go into service or become a dressmaker's apprentice and do these needlework services as paid employment. The sampler formed the basis of this learning phase. It was the practice piece with which to learn the skills and make a record of the techniques for future reference.

Plain sewing

'There was all the more time for me to hear old-world stories from Miss Pole, while she sat knitting, and I making my father's shirts. I always took a quantity of plain sewing to Cranford; for, as we did not read much, or walk much, I found it a capital time to get through my work.'

CRANFORD, Mrs Gaskell, 1853

Before sewing machines became commonplace, wives and daughters of modest homes were expected to sew all the family's undergarments, nightwear, shirts, aprons and caps. Only the ladies' dresses were ordered from the local dressmaker and the men's jackets, waistcoats and trousers from the tailor.

The sewing techniques required were learnt on a plain sewing sampler. These were seaming, hemming, gathering and tucking. Buttonholes, loops and making cloth buttons were essential skills, along with attaching tapes, frills, cuffs and creating gussets. Patching and repairing tears were important too and a few decorative stitches such as feather and herringbone could be used to decorate a hem or a collar.

The Workwoman's Guide, by a Lady, published in 1838, was a large volume dedicated to general needlework instructions. The first chapter deals with the necessary stitches, mending and darning. If a young lady had no relatives to turn to for instruction she would have found every topic described within these pages. Patterns for dress were included and although these would have dated, the general directions for children's clothes and underwear would have been useful until the end of the century.

Most plain sewing samplers date from the last quarter of the 19th century and were still produced up until the 1920s. Many were worked in schools and show the sweat and tears that were laboured over these scraps of cloth. The pupil-teacher was often in charge of needlework classes and she would have had to produce a perfect sampler to use as a teaching aid and to prove her ability and knowledge.

Plain sewing sampler
1870–1880
10 x 13¾in (25 x 35cm)

Stitches used on the plain sewing sampler.

Afine example of a plain sewing sampler, probably used for teaching purposes, worked on fine cotton fabric with pale blue, beige and pink cotton thread. It is signed with the initials M.M.

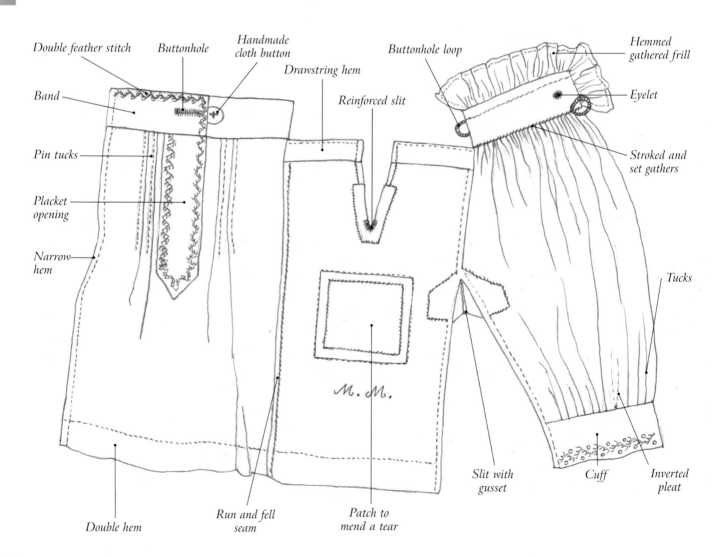

Double feather stitch · Buttonhole · Handmade cloth button · Drawstring hem · Buttonhole loop · Hemmed gathered frill

Band · Reinforced slit · Eyelet

Pin tucks · Stroked and set gathers

Placket opening

Narrow hem · Tucks

Slit with gusset · Cuff · Inverted pleat

Double hem · Run and fell seam · Patch to mend a tear

H Green's sampler

1886

7½ x 7½in (19.5 x 19.5cm), including the frill

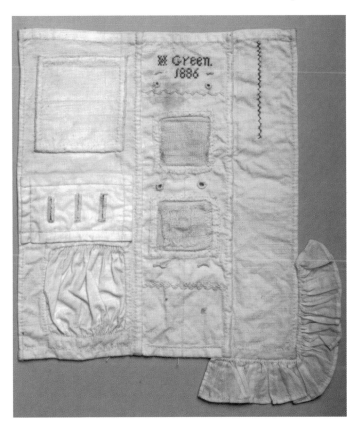

H Green's sampler, 1886.

A school sampler worked on coarse linen fabric. Crammed between two run and fell seams are the following techniques: hem stitched hems, buttonholes, a gathered patch, feather stitch, a knitted patch and a linen patch both with darns, loops for hooks, feather and chain stitch and the corner that has a muslin frill, which is whipped to the corner and hand hemmed. This young girl must have spent hours on this small scrap of fabric.

ES's sampler

1892

13¼ x 13in (34 x 33.5cm)

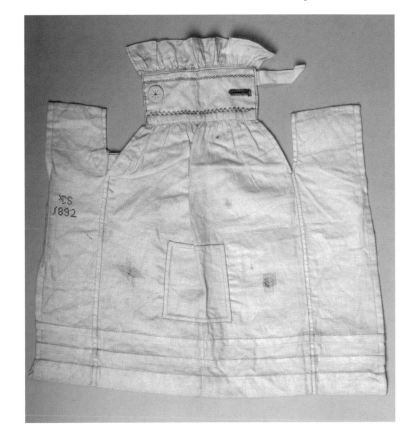

ES's sampler, 1892.

A child's sampler worked entirely in red thread on coarse linen fabric. The band at the centre is decorated with two types of feather stitch, a buttonhole and cloth button. It is finished with a muslin frill and an attached tape. The sides are joined with run and fell seams and demonstrate two slits, one reinforced with a gusset. There are two neat darns and a patch on the central piece and the whole is finished with two tucks and a double hem. Judging from the stains, this piece has caused a lot of sweat and tears!

Quarter-scale garments

Looking like doll clothes, another form of plain sewing sampler was made in the form of quarter-scale garments. These appear to have been made at an earlier date than the school samplers and would have been an excellent way of learning all the construction techniques without wasting a lot of fabric.

The favourite garments were men's shirts, nightshirts, drawers and pinafores. Accurate to the last detail they would have formed an excellent memory aid when stitching the full-scale garments.

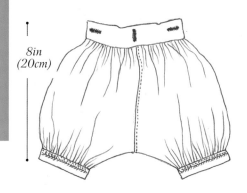

*8in
(20cm)*

Cotton pantaloons
circa 1870

THIS tiny garment is exquisitely hand-stitched with openings down the side seams. The waistband has five buttonholes, two at each side and one at the centre back. The legs are perfectly gathered on to the waistband and the cuffs, which are decorated with white feather stitch.

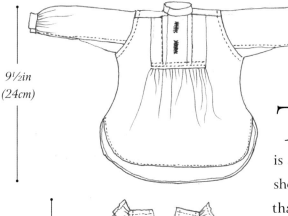

*9½in
(24cm)*

Linen shirt
circa 1820

THIS miniature garment is a man's shirt. The front panel has tucks either side of the placket opening and the collar is a straight, plain stand style. The narrow yoke on the shoulders control the gathers on the back, which is cut longer than the front. The sleeves are gathered into narrow cuffs.

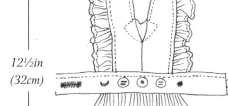

*12½in
(32cm)*

JMW's Linen apron
circa 1860

THE apron has many details, including a gusset slit at the neck and frill on the shoulders. The waistband has three handmade buttons sewn on by different methods, an eyelet, a stitched loop, a buttonhole and a tape attached to the end. The hem is finished with two tucks and a feather stitch and French knot border.

'Finally, – feeling as we do that ornamental needlework may be a charming occupation for those ladies whose happy lot relieves them from the necessity of 'darning hose' and 'mending night-caps', yet that a proficiency in plain sewing is the very life and being of the comfort and respectability of the poor man's wife...'

THE ART OF NEEDLEWORK, The Countess of Wilton, 1840

Stitches and techniques

Seaming

The most used seaming method was the run and fell. 'Fell' means hem in old English. It was durable and had the advantage that all the raw edges were enclosed and could not fray. For method see page 123.

Hemming

Unlike the modern slip stitched hem, the 19th century hem was more hardwearing and could be seen on the right side. A double hem was pressed and a small sloping, regularly spaced stitch was made through all the layers of fabric.

Buttons and buttonholes

Cloth buttons

Cloth buttons were made by gathering a circle of fabric around a metal ring. There were many delightful ways of decorating these buttons. The remaining thread in the needle could be used to sew the button on the garment and create a thread shank at the same time.

Buttonholes were harder wearing if they were sewn with the tailors' buttonhole stitch which had an extra twist.

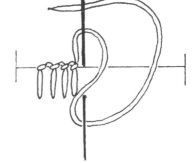

Tailors' buttonhole stitch

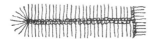

Buttonhole

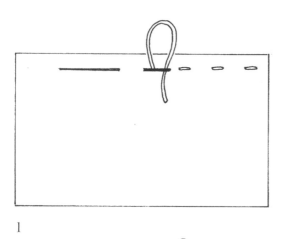

1

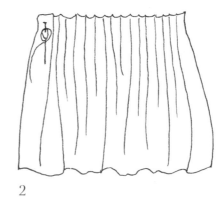

2

Gathering

Not many 19th century garments were without gathers so this was an essential technique that would be seen and admired.

1   The gathering was begun by working a line of running stitches along the edge of the fabric, leaving twice as much fabric between each stitch as was taken up by the needle.

2   The gathering thread was pulled up, to fit the band, and the surplus wrapped around a pin at the end. The piece was held top and bottom and pulled gently to put the gathers into position. The eye of the needle was used to 'stroke' each separate gather so they were evenly spaced.

3   The band was tacked in place and the setting stitch was worked in two stages. First the needle took a stitch in a horizontal position, catching the top of the gather.

4   Next a vertical stitch was made, catching the edge of the band.

3

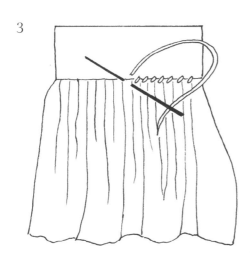

4

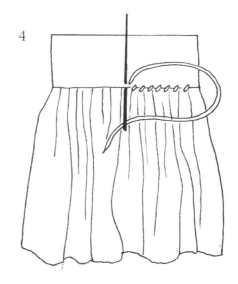

Marking and mending

If laundry services were to be used either outside the home or within a large country house, the household items and underclothes needed to be 'marked' with the owner's name and number. This was so that the freshly washed and ironed item could be returned to the rightful owner, checked against laundry lists and thus safeguarded against theft. As washday was a weekly or even a fortnightly event then the amount of items to be accounted for could be vast.

The task of marking all these garments and household linen fell to the women of the family and it was a task that could be given to quite young girls or the sewing maid. Working a simple alphabet sampler was the starting point. These samplers were usually small, made of evenweave linen and stitched with red or blue thread. The thread had to be purchased for the purpose so that the dye did not run or fade in the wash. The letters, upper and lower case and in different styles, were sewn on using a small cross stitch.

Pattern book, mid-19th century. Published by Heinrich Kuehn, Berlin, this folding book contains a dozen different alphabets and numbers in assorted styles.

'The marking of linen may be effected in a variety of stitches: Cross stitch, Embroidery stitches, and Chain stitch; but the orthodox style is after the first named method. ...To work: Procure ingrain red cotton, and work upon Linen of a coarse texture, so as to be guided by the threads that are woven in it.'

THE DICTIONARY OF NEEDLEWORK,
SFA Caulfield & BC Saward, 1885

These samplers were not stitched to learn the alphabet, although many were made in schools or orphanages. The techniques were learnt in preparation for young girls going into service. The samplers were made for practising marking and it is an endearing touch when the young embroiderer adds her name, the date and even her age. Little pattern books were available at the repositories and bookshops containing many different alphabets printed on graph paper. Some were in the form of folding booklets and often these were cut up and sold as single sheets.

Catherine Moss's alphabet sampler

1846

4½ x 4¼in (11.5 x 11cm)

This sampler is worked on exceptionally fine line, 32 threads per ³/₈in (1cm). It has an unusual composition with the letters in pairs over the numbers. Catherine filled the bottom of her sampler with the date, hearts and crosses and found the space for the warning quotation, 'If sinners entice thee consent thou not'.

Mary Anne Lauchlan's alphabet sampler

1850

7½ x 8¼in (19.5 x 21cm)

Aged only eight years, Mary worked this sampler in black and red cotton thread on linen woven with 14 threads per ³/₈in (1cm). The cross stitches are worked over two threads and the edge of the sampler is neatly hem stitched.

C Sander's alphabet sampler

1829

3½ x 3¾in (9 x 9.5cm)

This very small sampler is worked on fine linen, 24 threads per ³/₈in (1cm). It is worked in red and dark blue thread and the stitches are neatly worked. The hem stitched hem still has the tacking stitches in place.

Harriet Green's alphabet sampler

1830–1850

5¾ x 8½in (14.7 x 22cm)

Harriet's sampler was probably worked in school as it shows a few styles of letters. It is worked on a woollen fabric that has 16 threads per ³/₅in (1cm). The cross stitches are worked over two threads and the hem is neatly stitched and outlined in cross stitch.

Linen patches

'The mending of wearing-apparel and house and under-linen, though often ungrateful work is yet a necessity, to which every female hand ought to be carefully trained. How best to disguise and repair the wear and tear of use or accident is quite a valuable art as that of making new articles.'
ENCYCLOPEDIA OF NEEDLEWORK, Thérèse de Dillmont

Clothing and household linen was made to last in the 19th century and any worn areas or tears were carefully mended with a patch or a darn. Socks and stockings were also darned and likewise gloves and mittens.

The patch would be cut large enough to cover the hole and should match as close as possible in colour, texture and pattern. The patch was sewn 'straight to the thread' or on the same grain line as the fabric.

1 The patch was cut at least 2in (5cm) bigger than the hole and worn area. Then all the edges were turned in ¼in (6mm) and pressed. The patch was tacked in place, on the right side, and then neatly stitched around the edge using a small hem stitch.

2 The work was turned over and the worn area of the item was carefully cut away level with the patch's seam allowance. The raw edges were then blanket stitched together.

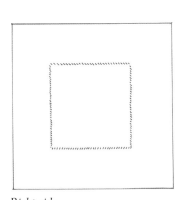

Right side

An alternative finish was to cut the patch's seam allowance narrower and turn the outside edge over this and hem stitch in place. All the raw edges would be enclosed and this would make a very durable patch for bed linen. A normal sharps sewing needle and cotton thread were used but linen thread would have been stronger.

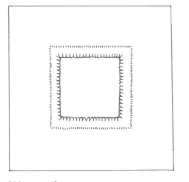

Wrong side

Darned patches

First the hole was trimmed to a regular shape, either a square, circle or rectangle. The hole was supported on the right side by tacking onto a piece of paper or in the case of stockings, over a darning egg.

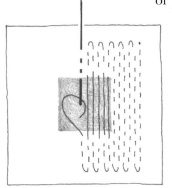

1 Working on the wrong side, the darning thread was woven under and over the fabric thread and across the hole in one direction. It was important that little loops were left at each turning and the stitches were not worked too tightly across the hole. The second stage of the darning took up any slack and washing could tighten the darn still further.

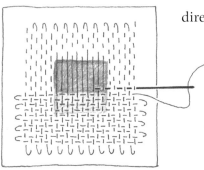

2 The darn was completed by repeating the stitching in the opposite direction, going under and over the 'warp' threads previously laid. Worked in a matching thread, the darn would be almost invisible.

A long thin needle, now known as a darning needle, would have been used. This would have reached across the darn to the other side and picked up the threads in one movement.

Dutch darning sampler

circa 1840

19 x 19¼in (48 x 48.5cm)

Detail of a twill-woven darn worked in a star shape.

DARNING samplers were usually worked in two or three colours of thread so that the intricate weaves could be seen clearly. This sampler is stitched in beige, mustard, yellow and brown threads and is worked on a linen ground of 16 threads per ³⁄₈in (1cm). The darns demonstrate the skills of creating plain weave, checks, stripes and twills. It also deals with mending holes, corner tears and slits. The whole sampler is set off with an unfinished cross stitch border.

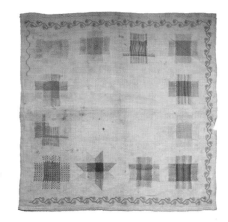

Decorative samplers

'*To make a sampler: Take some Mosaic Canvas of the finest make, and woven so that each thread is an equal distance apart. Cut this 18 inches wide and 20 inches long, and measure off a border all round of 4 inches. For the border, half inch from the edge, draw out threads in a pattern to the depth of half an inch, and work these with coloured silk; then work a conventional scroll pattern, in shades of several colours, and in TENT STITCH, to fill up the remaining 3 inches of border. Divide the centre of the Sampler into three sections. In the top section work a figure design. (In the old Samplers this was generally a sacred subject, such as Adam and Eve before the Tree of Knowledge.) In the centre section work an Alphabet in capital letters, and in the bottom an appropriate verse, the name of the worker, and the date.*'

THE DICTIONARY OF NEEDLEWORK, SFA Caulfield & BC Saward, 1885

Children created samplers following the above advice, in one form or another, throughout the 19th century. The alphabet bands could be placed at the top or in the middle. Motifs or scenes would fill the empty areas and the name and date were placed at the bottom. Traditionally, a repeating floral border attached to an undulating line surrounded the whole sampler.

The motifs, borders and alphabets were copied from patterns published expressively for sampler work. Little birds, trees in plant pots, floral borders, small animals and buildings occur in the same format on many samplers. These fanciful motifs are never found on the marking and mending samplers stitched by prospective working girls of the poorer families.

Verses were taken from the popular hymn books of the time and extracts from poetry books, which could supply a suitably pious quotation. Samplers dedicated to a deceased loved one were also popular.

As sampler stitching took up many hours of a young girl's time, it was seen as a means to keep a child occupied and out of mischief. Having been tutored by her governess or attended one of the new ladies' seminaries in the morning, a girl could then fill her afternoon with a brisk walk in the park and then a session on the sampler. It would never do for a child to be sat idle, particularly a girl.

Although some girls might have genuinely enjoyed needlework, many must have suffered nightmares about that dreadful piece of cloth appearing day after day. However, to sit and embroider was considered both decorous and the correct behaviour for the Victorian wife and her daughters.

Detail of the Adam and Eve panel.

Margaret Fraser's sampler.

Margaret Fraser's sampler

1818

12½ x 12¾in (32 x 32.5cm)

THIS brightly coloured sampler has all the requisite parts. There are three alphabets stitched in different sizes. Two are worked in cross stitch and the largest is embroidered in eyelet stitch. The wide carnation band is reminiscent of the previous century and below this there is a small scene of Adam and Eve confronting the serpent and the forbidden fruit.

Eliza Matilda Baynham's sampler

June 2nd 1813

12in x 15in (30 x 38cm)

THIS sampler epitomizes the ideal design with the delightful Georgian house placed in the central position. The ground is a very fine woollen cloth woven with 22 threads per ³⁄₈in (1cm). The cross stitch border is daintily stitched and there is a little scene of rabbits playing on the lawn worked in satin stitch on the bottom edge.

'The nearest approach thou canst make to Happiness on this side of the grave is to Enjoy from Heaven health and wisdom And peace of mind.'

Detail of the Georgian house.

Detail of the rabbits.

Decorative sampler stitches

Cross stitch

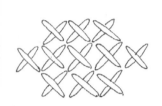

Usually the cross stitch was worked over two threads of the background fabric. It is personal choice as to which way the top stitch slopes but consistency meant neater work. When trying to stitch a very small script, cross stitch was worked over one thread. Unless carefully sewn, one half of the cross could slip behind the weave of the cloth and disappear.

Straight stitch

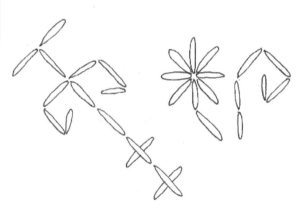

Straight stitches, again over two threads in any direction, were used for delicate stems and tendrils. Straight stitches worked from a central hole made tiny star shaped flowers.
If these were pulled tightly they formed a small eyelet, which was useful for the larger forms of alphabet.

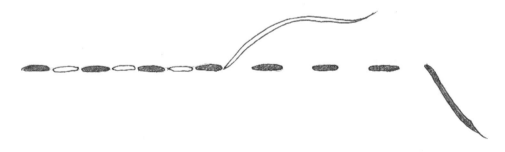

Double running stitch

Double running was used for single lines. One thread was used to go under and over two threads and another made a second journey or returned to fill the gaps. The second thread could be in a contrasting colour. This stitch is sometimes called 'Holbein' stitch because it was used for Elizabethan blackwork embroidery.

CASE STUDY

Combining learning with stitching

Elizabeth Page's map sampler
May 10th, 1811
Diameter 12in (30cm)

This map sampler is a lovely example of combining geography and history lessons with embroidering a sampler. In the centre of the map Spain and Portugal is featured. This area of Europe was much in the news at this time because of the Peninsular War, which lasted from 1808 until 1814.

In 1807, Napoleon had moved his French troops into Spain in order to invade Portugal. The next year, he deposed the Spanish monarch and put his own brother on the throne. Britain was Spain's ally and soon came rushing to her aid. In the following years there were many terrible battles throughout Portugal and Spain. Finally, the Duke of Wellington and the allies defeated Napoleon and after six harrowing years the Peninsular War was over.

The sampler is worked on fine gauze. The countries are outlined in double and triple rows of chain stitch and the names of the countries, regions and cities are embroidered with tiny cross stitches. A pretty floral border, also worked in chain stitch, surrounds the whole sampler. The sampler was originally mounted in a round, gold painted, wooden frame.

Detail of the floral border.

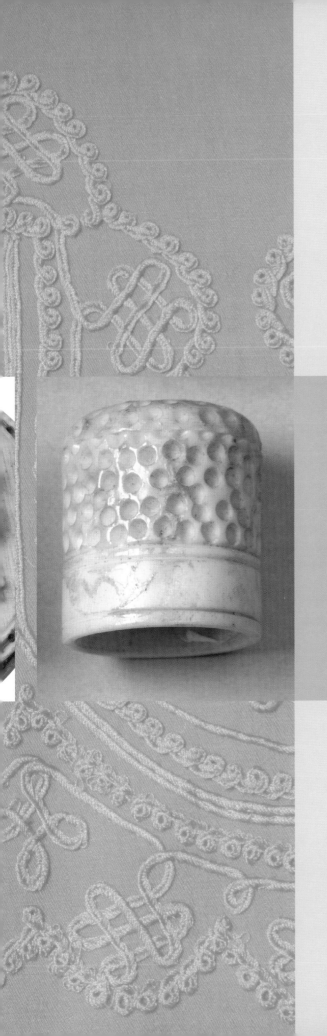

Needlework Tools & Cases

- ## *In the workbox*

'It is a good plan to fit up a square basket for the use of each working servant in the house...To these baskets should belong, a small tin box for buttons, hooks and eyes, bodkins, &c.; a large pair of scissors and sheath tied to each other... A heavy pincushion...A large needle-book. A bag to contain tapes, silks, darning cotton, & c.'

THE WORKWOMAN'S GUIDE, by a Lady, 1838

In the Workbox

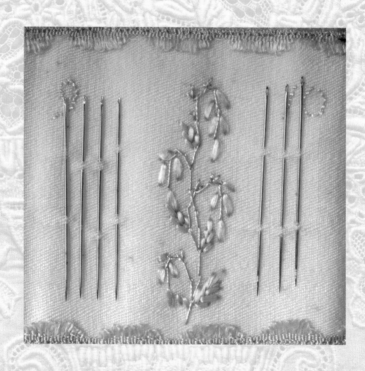

'A work-box, or basket, should be large enough to hold
a moderate supply of work and all its requisites, without being
of such a size as to be inconvenient to carry about, or lift
with ease. There should be in it divisions or partitions,
as they assist in keeping it in order; but some persons are apt
to run into the extreme of over-partitioning their boxes,
which defeats its own purpose and becomes troublesome:
this should be carefully avoided.'

THE WORKWOMAN'S GUIDE by a Lady, 1838

Workboxes and sewing cases

'A work box should contain six or eight of the useful sized white reel sewing cottons, black cotton, and silks, white, black, and coloured, both round and for darning; a few useful tapes, bobbin, galloon, buttons of all kinds, including thread, pearl, metal and black; also hooks and eyes. An ample needle-book, containing a page of kerseymere for each sized needle, not omitting the darning, glove, stay, and worsted or carpet needles. There are various kinds of scissors; the most useful are,

> *A large pair, for cutting out linen;*
>
> *A medium size, for common use;*
>
> *A small pair with rounded points;*
>
> *A smaller pair with sharper points, for cutting out muslin work, &c.;*
>
> *Lace scissors with a flat knob at one of the points;*
>
> *Button-hole scissors.*

A pincushion, an emery cushion, a waxen reel for strengthening thread, a stiletto, bodkins, a thimble, a small knife, and a yard measure, made like a carpenter's foot rule, only with nails instead of inches marked upon it.'

THE WORKWOMAN'S GUIDE by a Lady, 1838

The workbox described above would be for coping with all the household mending. However, 19th century ladies liked to take some dainty sewing tasks with them when they were travelling. Small sewing cases were called 'nécessaires' or 'lady's companions' and they held all the necessary equipment for light embroidery or a quick repair.

Leather lady's companion

1840–1890

Size 5¼ x 3½in (13.5 x 9cm)

THIS sewing case contains the basic sewing requisites and some cosmetic tools as well. There is a tape measure, thimble and pincushion, a stiletto and bodkin, a pair of sharp scissors and a penknife. There is also an earwax remover in the shape of a small spoon, with a pair of tweezers, for plucking eyebrows, at the other end. All the tools are beautifully made with filigree and modelled silver-gilt work. Some items may have been substituted due to loss or breakage but most are original.

Leather lady's companion.

A small hussif

1870–1890

9in x 5¾in (23 x 14.7cm)

A 'hussif' or 'housewife' was a folding case that contained all the necessities for emergency sewing. It was recommended as an essential item to pack for travel and was given to servicemen as part of their kit. The hussif usually contained a selection of needles and a bodkin, assorted threads, shirt buttons and a couple of hooks and eyes, scissors and a thimble.

This compact hussif is made of linen cloth. It has a narrow herringbone stitched line to hold a bodkin and a wide one to accommodate threads. Behind this section there is a pocket for other tools. A gathered thimble pouch is held together with smocking stitches. The large pocket at the end holds scissors and on the front there is a small needle case with two flannel leaves. The whole is decorated with feather stitching and silk bows. The back is plain purple silk fabric. The edges are machine-stitched and bound with matching silk ribbon. There is a ribbon at the pointed end to roll and tie the hussif for travelling.

Small hussif or 'housewife' made from linen cloth.

Tape measures and measurement

In *The Workwoman's Guide* it is mentioned that a yard measure marked out in 'nails' was necessary. All the patterns in this book were carefully drawn to scale and the measurements were given in nails, so that the needlewoman could reproduce them full size. The nail was the dressmaker's and tailor's unit of measurement until the middle of the 19th century when inches took over.

1 nail = 2¼in (5.75cm)

4 nails = 1 quarter = 9in (23cm)

4 quarters = 1 yard = 36in (91.5cm)

5 quarters = 1 English ell = 45in (114cm)

6 quarters = 1 French ell = 54in (137cm)

The yard, roughly measured by stretching the selvedge of the cloth from nose to fingertip, was accurately measured with a yardstick. It was broken down into smaller units by folding.

Fold the yard once to get half of a yard and again to get a quarter of a yard. Fold a quarter yard into four and the result is a nail of 2¼in (5.75cm). Hence a nail was 1/16 of a yard.

The English and French ells are still used today, although not recognized as such, as the fabric widths in the yardage information found on the back of modern dressmaking pattern envelopes.

Two 19th century tape measures.

Two 19th century tape measures

The drum-shaped wooden measure has a little handle to rewind the tape measure. It is marked in inches, which dates it from 1850 to 1860. Height 1in (2.5cm).

The bone container has a spindle fixed to the lid around which the silk tape measure is wound by hand. It is marked in nails, which dates it earlier than 1850. Height ¾in (2cm).

Paper pack of needles.

Needle cases and needle holders

The 19th century steel needles were of a very fine quality and there was more emphasis on using the correct size for a specific sewing job than is considered today. Needles were treasured and kept safe in homemade needle cases or in little containers made expressively for this purpose. Many such needle holders were bought as holiday souvenirs or given as presents.

Paper pack of needles

1850–1900

4 x 2½in (10 x 6.5cm)

Needles could be purchased in convenient sets, such as this little tartan folder containing sizes 6, 7 and 8 plus an assorted packet. On the opposite side there is a paper of pins. The pack neatly folds in two and fastens with a loop. Conveniently, there are a few glass-headed hatpins stuck in one end. By the 1840s, needles were much cheaper and people could afford to buy whole packets instead of one or two individual needles.

Blue tartan needle roll

circa 1840

14½ x 2½in (37 x 6.5cm)

This needle roll has five sections for needles numbered 5 to 9 and a couple of extra flannel leaves to hold bodkins and long darning needles. Each little flannel area has the size number sewn at the top and the sections are divided by four embroidered motifs. The pansies and forget-me-knots are embroidered in silk thread; the rose is made of ribbon work and the fuchsia stitched with chenille thread. The needle case rolls up and fastens with a button and loop.

Details of the embroidered flowers.

Blue tartan needle roll.

Pink silk needle roll

circa 1820

10½ x 2¼in (26.5 x 5.5cm)

THIS needle roll is made in a similar style to the tartan roll except the whole of the lining is made of cream flannel. The areas are divided up with little ribbon work motifs for needles numbered 6 to 11. There is a small pocket at the right-hand end to hold a thimble. The needle case rolls up and fastens with a pink silk ribbon.

Instructions for making a needle case

'Needlecase – This is made of a strip of kerseymere, one nail and a quarter wide, which is marked out in the required number of divisions, to separate the different sized needles from one another...The end of the strip is usually rounded,...and the initials worked on. Ribbons, or a button and loop are attached to the end, to fasten it up by.'

THE WORKWOMAN'S GUIDE, by a Lady, 1838

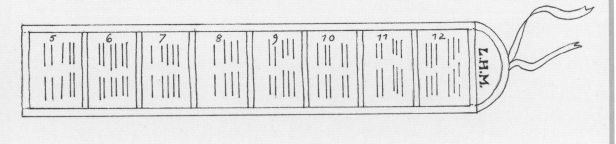

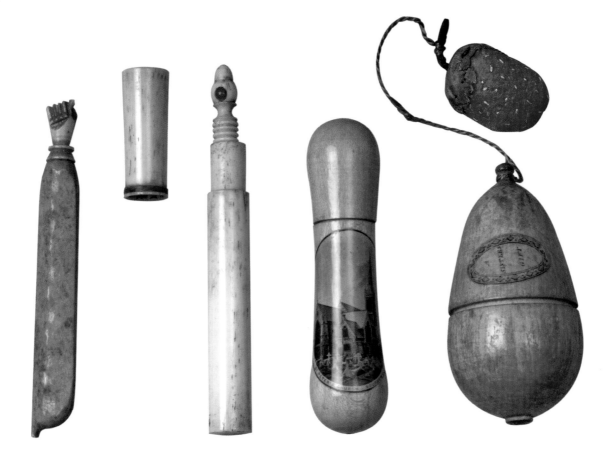

From left to right, peapod needle holder, bone needle case, souvenir needle case and pin poppet.

Purchased needle holders

The peapod needle holder, 1800–1820
3¼in (8.5cm) long

*The peapod is made of carved bone that is stained green.
It opens with a little screw top carved in the shape of a hand.*

Bone needle holder with a Stanhope, 1820–1850
3½in (9cm) long

*This plain little needle holder has a hidden secret. On removing
the lid, a tiny lens can be seen. When this is held close to the
eye, six scenes of Exeter can be viewed; the Cathedral and its
pulpit, the Guild Hall, Post Office and Albert Museum and
Exeter Bridge. All carefully printed in black ink with the
inscription 'A present from Exeter'.*

Holiday souvenir needle case, 19th century
3in (7.8cm) long

*This needle case is made of varnished wood and has an image of
St Peter's Church, Bournemouth. Such souvenirs were sold in
all the holiday towns in the 19th century.*

A pin poppet, 1800–1820
2¾in (7cm) long

*This pear-shaped wooden container could have held pins, needle
and a thimble. It has a little fabric strawberry attached to the
lid, which contains emery powder for sharpening needles.
The needle just needed to be stabbed into the strawberry a
couple of times to renew the point. The container has an
inscription on the side declaring 'A sister's gift'.*

Sewing birds

Sewing or hemming birds gave the 19th century needlewoman a third hand. They were clamped to the table about 8in (20cm) away from the needle position. The tail was pressed and the beak opened to hold the edge of the fabric. As the fabric was held at working height, the 'bird' exerted some tension to pull against and the hemming or seaming proceeded more quickly. The fabric was released, moved along and gripped again as the sewing progressed.

These clamps were called sewing birds because they were made of brass or bronze and usually cast in the shape of a bird. There were also simpler versions in the form of a plain spring clip. There was an alternative to the clamp and this was a heavily weighted pincushion. The edge of the work would be pinned to the cushion giving the same benefits.

'A heavy pincushion, formed of a brick or piece of iron or lead, placed in a bag full of bran, padded with flannel, and covered over with print or calico.'
THE WORKWOMAN'S GUIDE, by a Lady, 1838

Two sewing birds

1800–1860

6in (15cm) including the clamp

ONE is quite decorative and incorporates a pincushion on top. The other is a plain design but equally as useful. Sewing birds went out of fashion when the domestic sewing machine became commonplace in the home. There was no longer the need to sew long seams and hems by hand.

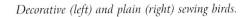

Decorative (left) and plain (right) sewing birds.

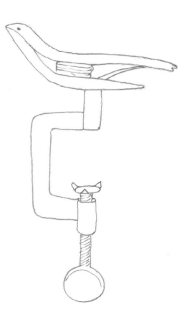

Historical threads

Needlework tools were often fitted with 'Stanhopes' or 'peeps' consisting of a tiny lens, less than $5/64$in (2mm) in diameter. The viewing side was very convex and thus had a high magnification. The other side was flat and on it was stuck a tiny picture, usually scenic views or architecture. They can be spotted by looking for a minute glass inset usually fixed in the lid or top of the tool. Lord Charles Stanhope, 1753–1816, invented this magnifying novelty.

A collection of stilettos made from bone and steel.

Stilettos or piercers

Pictured below is a collection of stilettos, some made of steel with bone handles and the others entirely bone. Apart from the obvious task of making holes in the cloth before stitching an eyelet, as for Broderie Anglaise, the bone stilettos could also be used as an improvised bodkin. A ribbon or tape was tied in one of the grooves and it could be threaded through a casing quite easily.

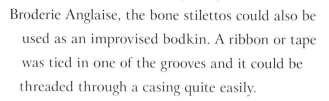

'A small sharply-pointed instrument, otherwise called a PIERCER forming one of the necessary appliances of a workbox...They best are of steel. It is employed for making eyelet holes in dressmaking, stay making, Embroidery, and for other purposes, and with the advantage of the preservation from tearing of the material, to which a cutting of the tissue would render it liable.'

THE DICTIONARY OF NEEDLEWORK, SFA Caulfield & BC Saward, 1885

Thimbles

It was always recommended that an old thimble be used for fine embroidery as it would have worn smooth and could not catch on the threads or fabric. Thimbles always had indentations on the top and sides to hold the eye end of the needle as it was pushed through the fabric. Very small thimbles are the ones worn by children.

A collection of brass and bone thimbles, 19th century.

'Thimbles are made in various sizes; and all common sorts are sold by the gross, but may be purchased singly. Gold thimbles are sometimes set round with turquoises and other gems. Those made of ebony, ivory and celluloid are very suitable for lace work. The former are known by the name of 'Nun's Thimbles'. Those of brass and steel are used by tailors and upholsterers, and by the working class in general.'

THE DICTIONARY OF NEEDLEWORK,
SFA Caulfield & BC Saward, 1885

Pincushions

Pincushions were often made as a token of friendship for girlfriends and gifts for aunts and mothers. Patterns for quite eccentric, miniature objects were in all the ladies' journals and magazines. Pincushions were an economical present to make as they only used the smallest scraps of fabric and a few beads as decoration.

Jockey's cap, pansy pincushion and bodkin holder.

A jockey's cap, 1880s
3¼ in (8cm) long

The stuffed jockey's cap is made of silk patchwork pieces and the brim and base is stiffened with card.

A pansy, 1880s
2¾ in (7cm) long

The pansy is made of silk and velvet cloth stretched over card. The two layers are stitched together to enclose all the raw edges. There is embroidered detail at the centre of the flower and on the leaves. The pins are pushed into the edges of the petals.

Bodkin holder, 1880s

Constructed in the same way as the pansy pincushion, the top has been left open to hold a metal bodkin.

Ivory and bone pincushions, 1800–1900
From 1¼in (3cm) to 2in (5cm) in diameter

A collection of ivory and bone pincushions.

Two flat bone discs are stitched together over felt padding through tiny holes drilled in the edge. The padding is covered with a pink silk ribbon. The pins were stuck into the sides.

The second decorated pincushion is made in the same way except that it is padded with sheep's wool and is trimmed with ribbon, although this has worn away with use. The pincushion with the floral carving is of the same construction and has purple silk ribbon around the sides.

The cylindrical cushion was once painted with red and green flowers. The ends are finished with gold-coloured velvet. One end is stuffed with wool and the other with emery powder.

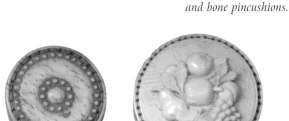

Glossary

Appliqué: cut fabric shapes applied to a background material and stitched in place.

Art Needlework: an embroidery design movement using naturalistic, flowing lines.

Arts and Crafts movement: a design movement associated with William Morris to shun mass-manufactured items and return to quality craftsmanship and design.

Ayrshire work: Scottish whitework embroidery stitched on fine cotton cloth incorporating needlepoint fillings.

Berlin wool work: stitching on canvas with brightly coloured wool threads from Berlin.

Bias: fabric cut at 45° to the weft and warp.

Blonde lace: a fine silk bobbin lace of a natural, undyed, cream colour.

Bodkin: a small pointed tool used to thread a ribbon through a casing.

Broderie Anglaise: whitework embroidery with eyelets and cutwork on cotton cloth.

Broderie Perse: a form of appliqué using motifs cut from printed cloth.

Carrickmacross work: Irish appliqué of muslin motifs applied to a net ground.

Chenille: a furry, silk embroidery thread.

Construction stitches: stitches used to hold garment pieces together, e.g. seams and hems.

Couching: stitches used to hold down a thick decorative thread, e.g. chenille or a metal thread.

Crash: a heavy linen fabric used for crewel embroidery.

Crewel wool: a two-ply, lightly twisted wool embroidery thread.

DMC (Dollfus-Mieg et Cie): a French manufacturer of embroidery and lace threads.

Ell: an old English linear measurement equal to 45in (114cm).

Florentine pattern: a zigzag or flame effect pattern worked in wool or silk on canvas.

Floss silk: a loosely twisted silk embroidery thread with a shiny finish.

Flounce: a decorative, gathered edging that is applied to the hem or edge of a garment.

Gauze: a very fine, silk, plain-weave fabric.

Grain line: the line of the warp threads on a piece of woven cloth.

Grisaille work: in embroidery terms, a monochromatic bead design worked on canvas.

Ground: the background fabric of an embroidered item; the areas left unstitched.

Guipure: a form of Carrickmacross work using bars or brides to connect the motifs.

Hussif: a small, roll-up needlework case that contains all the necessary sewing tools.

Insertion: a piece of lace or embroidery stitches used between two edges of fabric.

Interfacing: a layer of plain fabric used under a thin or unstable fabric to give a stronger base.

Laths: the lengths of wood that hold the rollers apart at the sides of an embroidery or quilting frame.

Liberty's of London: a popular department store that sold Arts and Crafts furniture, fabrics, clothes and Art Needlework materials.

Lining: a replica of the garment, made of an inferior or plain fabric, attached to the inside to conceal the construction stitches and the wrong side of any embroidery.

Mountmellick work: a form of Irish whitework worked with coarse cotton thread and featuring countryside motifs.

Muslin: a fine, plain woven cotton fabric, usually white in colour.

Nail: an old English linear measurement equal to 2¼ in (5.7cm).

Needlepoint: lace that is made with needle and thread.

Pastes: small glass jewels, on a spangle or a metal mount, that were stitched to the garment.

Penelope canvas: a double-weave canvas.

Petit point: fine tent stitch worked in every hole of a Penelope canvas.

Picots: small embroidered loops or knots that form a decorative edging to fabric.

Poonah brush: a flat-ended stencil brush.

Pounce: the powder used to transfer a design onto fabric via a pounce bag or a felt roll.

Pulled work: a form of embroidery where the stitches pull and distort the weave of the fabric to create decorative holes.

Sampler: either a collection of embroidery patterns or stitches, a child's embroidered picture or a practice piece to perfect a stitching technique.

Selvedge: the finished edge of a woven fabric running up both sides of the length.

Sharps needle: an ordinary dressmaking needle with a sharp point and a small eye.

Smooth: silk, metal or linen embroidery threads with a smooth, untwisted appearance.

Soutache work: narrow braid applied in a decorative and curving design.

Stanhope: a small magnifying glass found inserted in the end of needlework tools, through which a picture may be viewed.

Stiletto: a sharp, pointed tool used for piercing fabric to make eyelets.

Warp: the threads running the length of a woven fabric.

Webbing: a very strong tape used in upholstery or on the rollers of a slate embroidery frame.

Weft: the threads running from selvedge to selvedge of a woven fabric.

Whipping: a small sloping stitch worked over a cord or the raw edge of a fabric.

The Rachel Kay-Shuttleworth collections at Gawthorpe Hall
rbkscollection@tiscali.co.uk

Bibliography

ANONYMOUS, *Art Needlework, A Complete Manual*, Ward, Lock & Co., 1882

ANONYMOUS, *Embroidery on Muslin, Ladies Handbook*, HG Clarke & Co., 1843

ANONYMOUS (possibly E Masé), *Art Needlework, A Guide to Embroidery in Crewels, Silks & Appliqué & Etc*, The Home Help Series, Ward, Lock & Tyler, 1877

ARMES Alice, *English Smocks*, Dryad Press, 1977

BEETON Mrs, *Mrs Beeton's Book of Needlework*, Ward, Lock & Tyler, 1870

BOYLE Elizabeth, *The Irish Flowerers*, Ulster Folk Museum, 1971

BRADFIELD Nancy, *Historical Costumes of England*, Harrap, 1985

BRADFIELD Nancy, *Costume in Detail*, Harrap, 1968

BYRDE Penelope, *A Frivolous Distinction*, Bath City Council, 1979

CASSIN-SCOTT Jack, *The Illustrated Encyclopaedia of Costume and Fashion 1550–1920*, Blandford Press, 1986

CAULFIELD SFA & SAWARD BC, *The Dictionary of Needlework*, 2nd edition 1885, reprint, Blaketon Hall, 1989

CAVE Oenone, *Traditional Smocks and Smocking*, Mills & Boon Ltd, 1965

CHRISTIE Mrs Archibald H, *Embroidery and Tapestry Weaving*, John Hogg, 1915

CLABBURN Pamela, *The Needleworker's Dictionary*, Pitman Press, 1976

COLBY Averil, *Patchwork*, Batsford, 1958

DAWSON Barbara, *Whitework Embroidery*, Batsford, 1987

DILMONT Thérèse de, *Encyclopedia of Needlework*, reprint, Bracken Books, 1987

EDWARDS Joan, *Bead Embroidery*, Batsford, 1966

GROVES Sylvia, *The History of Needlework Tools*, Country Life Ltd, 1966

HALL Maggie, *Smocks*, Shire Publications, 1979

HEAD Carol, *Old Sewing Machines*, Shire Publications Ltd, 1982

HOUART Victor, *Sewing Accessories*, Souvenir Press, 1984

HOUSTON-ALMQVIST Jane, *Mountmellick Work*, Dryad Press, 1985

JACKSON Winefride, *The Royal School of Needlework, Yesterday and Today*, Anderson Blaby, 1982

JOHNSON Eleanor, *Needlework Tools*, Shire Publications Ltd, 1978

LADY A, *The Workwoman's Guide*, Simpkin, Marshall & Co., London, 1838

LOCKWOOD MS & GLAISTER E, A *Treatise on the Revived Practice of Decorative Needlework*, Marcus Ward & Co, London, 1878

MARSHALL Beverley, *Smocks and Smocking*, Alpha Books, 1980

MORRIS Barbara, *Victorian Embroidery*, Herbert Jenkins, 1962

MORRIS James A, *The Art of Ayrshire White Needlework*, Glasgow School of Art, 1916

MORRIS May, *Decorative Needlework*, Joseph Hughes & Co., London, 1893

NUNN Joan, *Fashion in Costume 1220–2000*, Herbert Press, 2000

QUILTER'S GUILD, *Quilt Treasures,* McDonald Books, 1995

PAINE Sheila, *Chikan Embroidery, The Floral Whitework of India*, Shire Press

PROCTOR Molly, *Victorian Canvas Work,* Batsford, 1972

ROTHSTEIN Natalie, *Four Hundred Years of Fashion*, Victoria & Albert Museum, 1984

SWAIN Margaret, *Ayrshire and Other Whitework,* Shire Publications Ltd, 1982

SWAIN Margaret, *The Flowerers, The Story of Ayrshire Needlework*, H Jennings & Co, 1955

SWIFT Gay, *The Batsford Encyclopaedia of Embroidery Techniques*, Batsford, 1984

THOMAS Mary, *Mary Thomas's Embroidery Book*, reprint, Hodder & Stoughton, 1983

THOMAS Mary, *Mary Thomas's Dictionary of Embroidery Stitches*, reprint, Hodder & Stoughton, 1974

WARDLE Patricia, *Guide to English Embroidery,* Victoria & Albert Museum, 1970

WARREN Geoffrey, *A Stitch in Time*, David & Charles, 1976

WELDONS, *Weldon's Needlework,* 1885

WELDONS, *Weldon's Shilling Guide to Fancy Work*, 1884, 1885

WELDONS, *Weldon's Practical Mountmellick Embroidery*, First Series, 1885

WILSON AN, *The Victorians*, Arrow Books, 2002

WILTON The Countess of, *The Art of Needlework*, Henry Colburn, 1840

YARWOOD Doreen, *Fashion in the Western World*, Batsford, 1992

The 19th century novels of :- Jane Austen, Anne Brontë, Charlotte Brontë and Mrs Elizabeth Gaskell

About the author

Friends would say that stitching, painting and drawing are almost an obsession for Gail. After studying Textile Design, specializing in Embroidery, at university, Gail's first post was that of the Curator of the Rachel Kay-Shuttleworth Collection at Gawthorpe Hall, Lancashire, north-west England. The collection consists of costume, embroidery, lace, woven and printed textiles from all over the world and provided a wonderful source for research, display and educational projects.

After a short break, raising a family, Gail went on to become a full-time teacher, passing her knowledge on to both school and university students. Often her historical knowledge would form the foundation for design projects integrating with a practical application of old and new techniques.

Now retired, Gail lives in a village on the Lancashire and North Yorkshire border in the north-west of England, continuing with her 'obsessions'. This is Gail's second book for GMC Publications and follows the highly successful *18th Century Embroidery Techniques*.

Acknowledgements

My sincere thanks go to the Trustees of the RBKS Collections for allowing me to use all the marvellous examples of 19th century embroidery.

Many thanks to the team at GMC, with a special mention for Virginia Brehaut, for a splendid working relationship.

Thank you to Martyn Pearson for the excellent photographs and his endless patience.

Lastly, a special thank you to my husband who read every word and, as he knows little about needlework, questioned any ambiguous instructions.

Index